Plumbing

& Heating

Albert Jackson and David Day

Hearst Books
A Division of Sterling Publishing Co., Inc.
New York

This work has been extracted from Popular Mechanics Complete Home How-To (copyright © 2004 by Hearst Communications, Inc.), published by Hearst Books, a division of Sterling Publishing Co., Inc., and originally published by HarperCollins Publishers under the title: Collins Complete DIY Manual—2nd edition, copyright © 2001 HarperCollins Publishers Ltd.

The written instructions, illustrations, and photographs in this volume are intended for the personal use of the reader and may be reproduced for that purpose only. Any other use, especially commercial use, is forbidden under law without the written permission of the copyright holder.

Every effort has been made to ensure that all the information in this book is accurate. However, in view of the complex and changing nature of building regulations, codes, and by-laws, the authors and publishers advise consultation with specialists in appropriate instances and cannot assume responsibility for any loss or damage resulting from reliance solely upon the information herein.

Popular Mechanics
Steve Willson, U.S. Project Editor
Tom Klenck, U.S. Art Director

Created, edited, and designed by Inklink
Concept, editorial, design and art direction: Simon Jennings
Text: Albert Jackson and David Day
Design: Alan Marshall
Illustrations: David Day, Robin Harris, Brian Craker, Michael Parr, Brian Sayers
Photographs: Paul Chave, Peter Higgins, Simon Jennings, Albert Jackson

Hearst Books
Project editor: Joseph Gonzalez

Library of Congress Cataloging-in-Publication Data
Jackson, Albert, 1943-
  Popular Mechanics plumbing & heating / Albert Jackson and David Day.
      p. cm.
  Includes bibliographical references and index.
  ISBN-13: 978-1-58816-531-2 (alk. paper)
  ISBN-10: 1-58816-531-0 (alk. paper)
  1. Plumbing—Amateurs' manuals. 2. Dwellings—Heating and ventilation—Amateurs' manuals. I. Day, David, 1944- II. Popular Mechanics Press. III. Title.
  TH6124.J34 2006
  696'.1—dc22
                                                    2006001725

10 9 8 7 6 5 4 3 2 1

Published by Hearst Books
A Division of Sterling Publishing Co., Inc.
387 Park Avenue South
New York, NY 10016

Popular Mechanics and Hearst Books are trademarks of Hearst Communications, Inc.

www.popularmechanics.com

For information about custom editions, special sales, premium and corporate purchases, please contact Sterling Special Sales Department at 800-805-5489 or specialsales@sterlingpub.com.

Distributed in Canada by Sterling Publishing
c/o Canadian Manda Group, 165 Dufferin Street
Toronto, Ontario, Canada M6K 3H6

Printed in China

Sterling ISBN-13: 978-1-58816-531-2
        ISBN-10: 1-58816-531-0

Contents

Today, more and more homeowners are willing to tackle their own plumbing repair and remodeling projects. As with most do-it-yourself endeavors, cost is a motivating factor. The lion's share of most plumbing bills is the cost of professional labor, so doing your own repairs and installations makes good economic sense, and offers as a bonus the satisfaction of greater self-sufficiency.

Fortunately for the do-it-yourselfer, the plumbing supply industry has wasted no time in recognizing the opportunities provided by the growing consumer market. In addition to selling plumbing supplies in bulk quantities to wholesale houses and plumbers, manufacturers are now marketing for the consumer as well. They are also making their products easier to use. Repair and replacement parts are now likely to be attractively packaged with instructions and a "you can do it" pep talk on the back of each blister pack.

To the further benefit of the homeowner, design and manufacturing trends have also steered the industry in the direction of lighter, less-expensive, and easier-to-install materials. City code authorities have recognized the need to make plumbing more affordable in new construction and have adjusted their material requirements accordingly.

The upshot of all of this is that basic plumbing has never been easier and has never required so few specialized tools. Still, the most important ingredient in any do-it-yourself project is confidence. Confidence starts with a basic understanding of how plumbing works and increases with every project your complete.

If you own your home, you can work on any of its plumbing. Your work will have to meet accepted plumbing standards as defined by local code regulations. Plumbing codes are written and enforced locally in the United States, but are based on specifications of the national Uniform Building Code. Before starting any major plumbing project, check with your local code office to see if the work you have planned meets specific code requirements.

A typical plumbing system

A residential piping system can be divided according to function into five basic categories. These categories are: pressurized water and fuel pipes, gravity-flow soil pipes, vent pipes, fixtures, and appliances. All pipes in a system serve specific fixtures (sinks, lavatories, and tubs) and appliances (water heaters, disposers, dishwashers, and clothes washers).

Take time to familiarize yourself with this network of pipes in your home before beginning any repair or remodeling project.

An understanding of how each component in your system works with other components will help you feel more confident about the project at hand. Think about each pipe, valve, and fixture in your home as it fits within one of the five basic categories of function. Consider each item within the system separately. Until each element is examined according to its use, the system as a whole will likely remain a mystery. Plumbing is best learned one step at a time.

PLUMBING SYSTEM

① Water service
Water supply from water company.

② Water meter
Records water usage.

③ Cold-water supply
Carries cold water to fixtures and appliances.

④ Sillcock
Cold-water access from outside house.

⑤ Gas line
Gas supply from gas company.

⑥ Water heater
Heats water for fixtures and appliances.

⑦ Hot-water supply
Carries hot water to fixtures and appliances.

⑧ Supply riser
Water connection just below fixture.

⑨ Drain and trap
Carries waste from fixture or appliance.

⑩ Main drain
Carries waste from all fixtures and appliances.

⑪ 3-in. stack
Main vent for entire waste system.

⑫ Vent
Individual vent for fixture or appliance.

⑬ Cleanout
Access to waste system to remove blockages.

⑭ Floor drain
Carries water from basement floor.

⑮ 4-in. soil pipe
Carries house waste to public sewer system.

Supply lines

The water that flows from your tap enters your home through a single water-service pipe. This pipe is buried below frost level in your yard and extends from the city water main to a meter valve just inside your home. If water is supplied from a well, it flows to a pressure tank, where it is stored until needed. In some cases, the water meter will be located in a meter pit just outside the home.

The water service is then connected to a meter, which measures the amount of water you use. From the meter, a single trunk line, carrying cold water, usually travels up and along the center girder of a home. At convenient intervals along the way, smaller branch lines extend from the trunk line to service various fixtures throughout the house. One goes to the water heater which supplies hot water to another trunk. This hot trunk line usually travels side by side with the cold line and branches off to wherever hot water is needed.

SUPPLY COMPONENTS

1 Water main
The water company uses this pipe to carry water to all the homes in the neighborhood.

2 Corporation stop
This valve is used to shut off water supply at the water main.

3 Curb stop
This valve shuts off water supply just before it enters the house.

4 Iron cover
This cover gives access to the curb stop at grade level.

5 Meter stop
This valve shuts off water before it reaches the meter. This makes replacing the meter much easier.

6 Meter
The meter records water consumption for water-company billing.

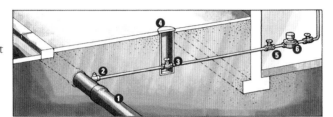

Drainage and venting

Drainage lines are the pipes that carry soiled water from your fixtures to the public sewer system. They generally consist of one or more vertical stacks with horizontal drains attached. It is important that drainage lines are installed at just the right pitch. Too little fall will cause water and solids to drain sluggishly and may cause the line to clog. Too much fall, particularly on long runs, will cause the water to outrun the solids, which may also cause the line to clog. A fall of ¼ inch per foot is ideal.

As a public sewer system is vented through the roofs (via plumbing stacks) of the homes connected to it, sewer gas is always present in large quantities in drainage systems. Each fixture must therefore have a seal to keep noxious sewer gases from entering the home through fixture drains. This seal is created by a U-shaped pipe, called a trap, beneath each fixture. Traps allow water to pass through them when a fixture is drained. After a fixture is drained, however, the trap holds a measured amount of water in its bend so that sewer gas cannot pass through the pipe and into your home. Every fixture in your home must have a trap, and every trap must be vented.

Venting is one of the most critical aspects of a drainage system. Without correctly vented drain lines, toilets won't flush properly, sink and lavatory drains choke, and high-volume appliance drains may overflow. But most important, unvented drain lines siphon water from fixture traps. Once a trap seal is broken, sewer gas quickly enters your living quarters. Even in quantities too small to detect by smell, sewer gases can cause respiratory problems and headaches.

The type of vent used depends upon the number of fixtures and floor levels involved and the structural constraints peculiar to each home.

DRAINS AND VENTS

1 Soil stack
This is the main waste line in the house. It directs all the waste from fixtures and appliances to the sewer line, or septic-system line, outside the house.

2 Main vent stack
This pipe carries sewer gases from the system into the air above the house. It also serves to equalize the air pressure in the system.

3 Vent line
The vents carry sewer gases from the fixtures and appliances and equalize the air pressure in the waste system.

4 Trap
This fitting contains water to keep sewer gases from entering the house.

5 Drain line
These pipes capture waste from the fixtures and appliances and carry it to the soil stack.

6 Cleanout
This fitting provides access to the waste system for removing blockages with a plumber's snake or drain auger.

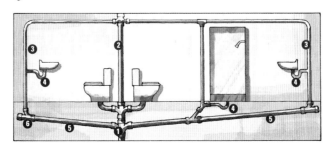

Draining a water system

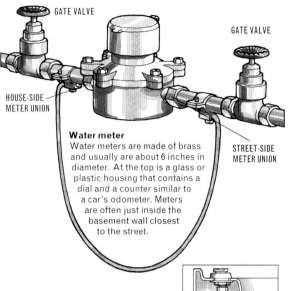

GATE VALVE

GATE VALVE

HOUSE-SIDE
METER UNION

Water meter
Water meters are made of brass
and usually are about 6 inches in
diameter. At the top is a glass or
plastic housing that contains a
dial and a counter similar to
a car's odometer. Meters
are often just inside the
basement wall closest
to the street.

STREET-SIDE
METER UNION

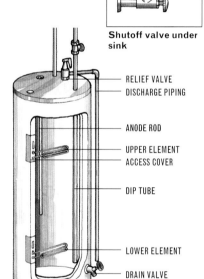

**Shutoff valve under
sink**

RELIEF VALVE
DISCHARGE PIPING

ANODE ROD

UPPER ELEMENT
ACCESS COVER

DIP TUBE

LOWER ELEMENT

DRAIN VALVE

**Open faucets to bleed air when recharging
system**

Being able to locate and shut off your meter valve or, if you live in the country, your pump switch is an important homeowner responsibility. You must be able to act quickly in an emergency.

Draining the system

To drain your water system, first shut off the valve on the street side of the meter. Then shut off the valve on the house side of the meter. With both valves closed, place a bucket under the meter and loosen the meter union next to the house-side valve. The small amount of water trapped in the meter will trickle through the opened union. Then go through your house and open all faucets to prevent air lock. When these are open, return to the basement and open the house-side valve and slowly drain the water into a bucket.

Partial drain-downs

In many instances, such as toilet repairs, there will be no need to drain the entire system. A toilet usually has a shutoff valve between the riser and the supply line under the tank. Some homes have shutoff valves under sinks and lavatories as well. When these valves are present, use them. It is almost always easier to isolate a single fixture than to put the entire system out of order.

Draining your water heater

There can be several reasons why you might want to drain your water heater. The most likely occasion will be when removing an old heater. Sediment, faulty electrical elements, and stuck relief valves are three other common problems that require draining.

Start by shutting off the water supply to the heater. If your heater has a cold-water inlet valve, use it and leave the cold-water side of the system on. If no inlet valve is present, you will have to shut down the water supply to the entire house at the meter.

Once water to the heater is shut off, open all hot-water faucets in the house to prevent air lock. Then, attach a garden hose to the drain valve and empty the tank. If yours is an electric heater, an added precaution: Energized electrical elements burn out in a matter of seconds when not immersed in water, so you must shut off the power to the heater before draining it.

Recharging the system

Just as you opened all faucets to prevent an air lock when draining the system, you will need to open them to bleed air from the lines when recharging the system with water. Open the meter valves only partway. Then bleed the air from the newly charged lines. After all the air in the system has escaped through the faucets, turn the faucets off and turn the meter valves all the way open. Small bursts of air may still escape through your faucets when you first use them, but all the air should be dissipated after the first full pressure draw. If you do not bleed trapped air from supply lines, the shock of air released under full pressure could damage faucet and supply-pipe seals.

It seems that plumbing leaks occur when we are least prepared to deal with them, at night, during the winter, when we're away from home, or just about always on a weekend. In such cases, a plumber may not be readily available, and you may not have the time and materials on hand, or the expertise for that matter, to make a permanent repair. There are, however, a number of stopgap measures that you can use to repair leaks temporarily. And most of them make good use of commom materials that just about all of us have on hand around the house.

Frozen and split pipes

In colder climates, pipes located in exterior walls, crawl spaces, and attics are often subject to freezing. The best preventive measure is to insulate these pipes. Even insulated pipes, however, can freeze when exposed to drafts of extremely cold air. When pipe freezes, a plug of ice forms in a small section of the pipe and expands against the pipe walls. The expansion swells the pipe and, in most cases, ruptures the pipe wall.

Frozen water can easily split even the best copper pipe

Even a well-protected pipe may crack after years of use. Factory defects and corrosion are often responsible for these leaks. Regardless of how a pipe cracks or splits, emergency repair methods are usually the same.

A sure sign that a pipe has frozen is that no water passes through the pipe to the faucets nearest the freeze. You will often be able to feel along the pipe and locate the frozen area. If the pipe has not yet ruptured, use a portable hair dryer to warm the frozen area until water again

Repair coupling
This kit uses a rubber sleeve and a hinged metal clamp.

flows to the nearest faucet. Once the pipe has thawed, you should wrap it with insulation. If no insulation is available, use old rags and fasten them to the pipe with tape, string, or wire.

If you can see that the pipe has already split, you will need to drain the system before thawing the frozen area. Once the area has thawed, you will need to make some sort of emergency repair. If you are able to find a plumbing-supply outlet, the best solution is to buy a sleeve-type repair coupling. These couplings can be purchased in a number of standard sizes. They consist of two metal halves that are hinged on one side and bolted together on the other. A rubber sleeve fits inside and wraps completely around the pipe.

To install a sleeve repair coupling, first clean the pipe with a wire brush or sandpaper. Then fit the rubber sleeve around the pipe so that the seam is opposite the leak. Fit the metal halves of the collar over the sleeve and tighten the two halves together. While this method is usually thought of as an emergency repair, if the area has been properly prepared, it can be permanent.

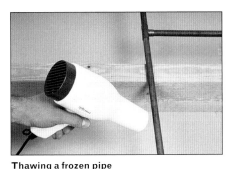

Thawing a frozen pipe
Move a hair dryer back and forth across the frozen pipe until the water starts to flow again.

If conventional repair materials are not available, you can sometimes make do with materials found around the house or at your local all-night service station.

To create a makeshift sleeve coupling, use a piece of tire inner tube, or a section of old garden hose, and a few radiator hose clamps. Wrap the inner tube around the split pipe several times and clamp it in place with hose clamps. This is at best a stopgap measure, but it will slow the leak until you can make a more permanent repair.

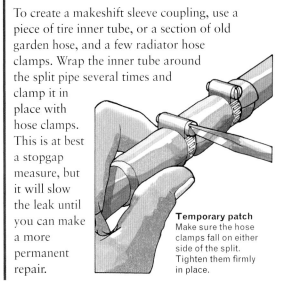

Temporary patch
Make sure the hose clamps fall on either side of the split. Tighten them firmly in place.

Epoxy patch repair

If you do not have access to plumbing materials, you may still be able to buy a general-purpose epoxy kit. These kits consist of two sticks of putty that you knead together. Once the parts are completely mixed, you will have about fifteen minutes to work before the mixture begins to set. Start by cleaning and drying the area around the split with sandpaper and alcohol. Knead the two components until they are a single consistent color and begin to give off heat. Then press the epoxy putty around the pipe. Smooth the ends with a damp cloth until the epoxy forms a seamless bond around the pipe extending several inches on either side of the split.

Epoxy takes a full 24 hours to cure, but, after a few hours, you should be able to turn the water on slightly. Do not put full pressure in the pipes for at least 24 hours after applying an epoxy patch.

Epoxy patch
Must cure properly before turning on water.

3-in. PVC pipe

1½-in. PVC pipe

1½-in. banded coupling

3-in. sanitary tee with 1½-in. side inlet

1½-in. standard sanitary tee

1½-in. 90° ell

1½-in. wye

1½-in. 45° street ell

Male adapter

Standard glue-joint coupling

Adjustable plastic toilet flange

Female insert adapter

Working with plumbing pipe is better today than it was thirty years ago, largely because of plastic and copper. Both are much easier to work with than their predecessors, cast iron and steel. And both are highly resistant to corrosion.

Waste pipe and fittings

Shown here are common residential drainage and vent pipes and fittings. Others are available to solve specific problems. And most come in diameters from 1½ in. to 4 in.

3-in. and 1½-in. PVC pipe
Used for drain and vent lines.

3-in. sanitary tee with 1½-in. side inlet
Feeds 3-in. toilet waste line and 1½-in. shower drain into main stack.

1½-in. wye
Has less severe 45-degree inlet angle than a standard 1½-in. tee.

1½-in. standard sanitary tee
Most often used as a dry-vent fitting above the highest wet-drainage fitting.

1½-in. 45-degree street ell
Used in close quarters, the fitting has one male end and one hub end.

1½-in. 90-degree ell
Standard elbows have female hub on both ends.

Male adapter
For joining plastic pipe to female pipe threads, usually on iron, brass, or copper pipe.

Female insert adapter
For joining plastic pipe to male pipe threads, usually on iron, brass, or copper pipe.

Standard glue-joint coupling
For joining two pipes with solvent cement.

1½-in. banded coupling
Can join plastic pipe to cast-iron, copper, brass, and chrome pipe. Consists of a rubber sleeve, stainless-steel band, and two hose clamps.

Adjustable toilet flange
For joining a toilet bowl to the waste piping and the bathroom floor.

Supply pipes and fittings carry potable water throughout the house. Rigid copper pipe and copper and brass fittings have long been the standards for residential water systems and will likely remain so because of their durability. The pipe and fittings shown here are the most common components used for residential water supply systems.

Copper pipe, ¾- and ½-in.
Standard water supply pipes. The ¾-in. pipe is used for main trunk lines. The ½-in. pipe is used for branching off to individual fixtures.

Soft copper tubing, ⅜-in.
Most often used for riser pipes between supply lines and fixtures. Available in other sizes for other jobs.

Prefitted stainless-steel risers
Flexible pipes that join shutoff valves under sinks and toilets to the fixtures.

Tees, ells, street ells, and couplings
Standard fittings for copper pipe. Available in ½- and ¾-in. diameters, they are joined to pipe with solder. Other specialized fittings are available for unusual situations.

Male adapter
Most often used to join copper pipe to threaded fittings on water meters, heaters, and softeners.

Dielectric union
For joining copper pipe to steel pipe. Prevents electrolytic corrosion between dissimilar metals.

Brass union
Provides a mechanical, instead of soldered, joint between pipes so they can be quickly disassembled.

Ball valve
In-line valve that allows full flow—no water restriction—when open.

Boiler drain
A compression valve, often used to connect supply lines with washing-machine supply hoses.

Chrome compression valve
Standard shutoff valve for under sinks and toilets.

¾-in. tee   45° standard ell   90° street ell   Slip coupling

¾-in. copper pipe

½-in. copper pipe

¾-in. male adapter   Dielectric union   Brass union

⅜-in. soft copper tubing

Ball valve   Boiler drain   Chrome compression valve

Prefitted stainless-steel risers

Hanging accessories

Code requirements stipulate that horizontal pipes must be supported every 4 to 6 feet, depending on pipe size. There are a variety of hangers for getting this job done. Two of the most common are shown on the right.

Plumber's strap
This perforated strapping is very flexible and comes in rolls, so you just cut what you need for the job at hand. The holes make it easier to nail or screw the strap to floor joists. It is particularly useful for large drain and vent pipes.

Copper two-hole strap
These straps are sized for the pipe being supported, usually ½- or ¾-in. diameter. They are nailed or screwed to wood framing members.

Plumber's strap

Copper two-hole strap

Working with pipe

General piping considerations

Until you learn to work with pipe, your plumbing capabilities will be limited to simple maintenance. While neoprene gaskets, no-hub couplings, and plastic pipe and fittings have greatly reduced the need for special knowledge and specialized tools, most remodeling still requires that you understand how traditional plumbing materials are put together. In most cases, these newer, easier-to-use materials will have to be tied into existing pipes. You may also need to dismantle some existing piping in order to repair or extend your plumbing system. In short, knowing how to use plastic pipe is of little use if you do not also know how to tie it to other kinds of pipe in your existing system.

The good news is that the skill needed to work with cast-iron, steel, and copper pipe has been seriously overrated. You can do it. You may need a few specialized tools, but you can rent those. What is necessary is a basic understanding of how these materials are put together and which fittings and tools make the job easier. The rest is a matter of practice.

Making the connection

With the acceptance of plastic as a plumbing material, several new methods of joining plastic to conventional soil pipe have been developed. These connectors have virtually eliminated the skill once needed to form mechanical joints. Where once molten lead and oakum (an oily, ropelike material) were packed into bell-and-spigot joints, now neoprene gaskets make the seal. Instead of dismantling a run of pipe all the way back to its nearest hub, you can join two hubless pipes in minutes with no-hub couplings.

Bell-and-spigot gaskets
Neoprene gaskets are made for every standard-size, cast-iron soil pipe. They are fitted rubber collars that snap into the bell of a cast-iron pipe. The inside of the gasket is then lubricated with detergent (e.g., dish soap), and the male end of the adjoining pipe is forced into the gasket until it seats.

No-hub couplings
No-hub couplings are rot-resistant rubber sleeves with stainless-steel bands around them. They are designed for use on drainage pipes and are approved by most code authorities. To install no-hub couplings, you simply slide one end of each pipe into the sleeve and tighten the bands. No-hubs come in many sizes, including increasing and decreasing couplings that allow you to join different pipe sizes to one another. They are particularly handy in joining dissimilar pipe materials.

When installing drainage pipe, follow these rules to ensure mechanically sound joints and even-flow patterns:
1. The grade or elevation of a drainage pipe should not be less than $\frac{1}{16}$ inch per running foot of pipe. In total, the fall of a given pipe run should not be greater than the diameter of the pipe involved. For example, a 2-inch pipe should not drop more than 2 inches along its entire length. If structural constraints require that a pipe drop more than its diameter, fittings should be used to "step" the pipe down to a lower plane. In this case, a vent will be required before stepping down.
2. When drainage pipes are wet, or carry water, use fittings with gradual flow patterns. For example, tees should be used only when they are the highest fittings on a vertical pipe. Never use them in horizontal positions or when other fixtures are served above them. Because wyes offer much more gradual-flow patterns, they should always be used instead of tees, except as the highest branch fitting on a vertical stack.
3. When drainage pipes are suspended from floor or ceiling joists, they should be supported by pipe hangers at a rate of at least one every 6 feet, or one for every pipe less than 6 feet long.
4. Every vertical stack must have a cleanout fitting at its base before entering a concrete floor.
5. All pipes installed underground or under concrete must be laid on even, solid soil. No voids or low spots are allowed under a pipe. If voids exist, or if the grade has been overexcavated, the ditch should be lined with fill sand. Never fill voids or raise a pipe with soil. As soil settles, it will cause the pipe to sag and clog, or to shear off entirely.

When excavating a ditch for soil pipe, dig a small impression in the soil for each pipe hub. This will keep the entire length of the pipe from resting only on the hubs. Because soil pipe is buried permanently, either underground or under concrete, always work for a permanent installation.

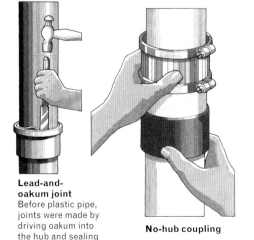

Lead-and-oakum joint
Before plastic pipe, joints were made by driving oakum into the hub and sealing it with molten lead.

No-hub coupling

Drain and vent sizing

FIXTURE	DRAIN SIZE	VENT SIZE	MAX. LENGTH TO STACK
Toilet	4"	2"	10'
Toilet	3"	2"	6'
Sink	1½"	1½"	3'6"
Lavatory	1½"	1½"	3'6"
Tub	1½"	1½"	3'6"
Shower	2"	1½"	5'
Laundry	2"	1½"	5'
Floor drain	2"	1½"	5'

Plastic drainage pipe

Plastic pipe is the easiest pipe to handle because it is lightweight, can be cut with a hacksaw, and is joined to its fittings with glue. Plastic drainage pipe comes in two forms. ABS pipe is black and PVC is white. Both are schedule #40 weight, which is the wall thickness required by code for drainage pipe. There is no appreciable difference between the two, except that ABS has become more expensive in recent years, and the plumbing industry in general seems to be moving away from it. For consistency, you should match the type already in your home.

Joining plastic to iron

Plastic drainage pipe can be joined to cast-iron pipe in two ways. One is to cut the cast iron with a rented snap cutter and then join the pipes with a no-hub, or a banded, coupling. The other is to use a neoprene gasket.

To do this, buy a gasket that matches the size of the pipe being joined. Then push it into the cast hub and lubricate it with some dishwashing liquid to make joining the pipes easier. File over the sharp edge on the end of the plastic pipe and firmly push the pipe into the gasket.

Cut cast-iron pipe with rented snap cutter

Push neoprene gasket into hub, followed by pipe

Cutting and assembling

To cut and fit plastic pipe, measure for the desired length and mark the pipe with a pencil. Then, using a hacksaw, cut carefully across the pipe **(1)**. Take particular care in making straight cuts. A crooked cut will keep the end of the pipe from fitting properly into the hub of the fitting. Smooth the cut edge with a file **(2)**.

It is always a good idea to assemble pipe and fittings before gluing to make sure that all measurements are accurate and all fitting angles correspond. Then, before dismantling, mark the fitting and pipe **(3)** at each joint so that you will have an easy reference point when gluing them together permanently. You can also scratch a mark with a utility knife **(4)**. This won't smear as pencil marks often do.

Gluing pipe and hubs is easy but requires accuracy and speed. Apply glue to the inside of the hub of the fitting. Then glue the outside of the pipe, covering to a depth consistent with the depth of the hub **(5)**. Press the fitting onto the pipe with the pencil marks about an inch apart. When the pipe is in all the way, turn the fitting so that the pencil marks line up. By turning the fitting on the pipe, the glue is spread out evenly around the entire joint.

Glued joints (technically, cemented joints) set in about 30 seconds, so if you make a mistake, you have to pull the joint apart very quickly. Plastic pipe cement does not really glue one surface to another; rather, it melts the two surfaces, causing them to fuse. Once a joint has set, it is permanent.

When buying materials, be sure to choose a cement made for the type of pipe you buy. ABS glue will not cement PVC pipe and fittings. PVC glue does work with ABS pipe, so you have to use compatible materials.

Drainage pipe must often be installed in interior walls. Because plastic pipe expands and contracts with hot and cold water, make sure that holes drilled in the wall studs are large enough to allow for this expansion. Stud and joist holes should be at least ⅛ inch larger than the exterior diameter of the pipe. Plastic pipe should never be shimmed tightly against wood. Without room for expansion, plastic pipe will produce an annoying ticking sound in the wall after hot water has been drained through.

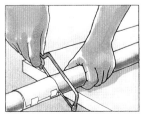

1 Use paper as a guide to keep the cut square

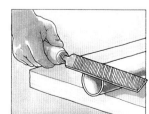

2 Smooth the end with a file

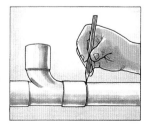

3 Preassemble the joint and mark pipe and fitting

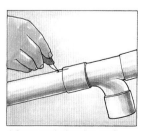

4 Or scratch the pipe and fitting with a knife

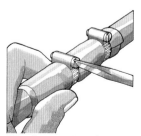

5 Brush cement on pipe end and fitting hub

Plastic water pipe

Connecting metal to plastic pipe

Joining **CPVC** plastic pipe to fittings

CPVC (chlorinated polyvinyl chloride) plastic water pipe has been used for water-supply lines in some parts of the country for many years. If installed properly, it's got a good track record. And there is no question that it's easier to work with than rigid copper pipe and fittings. No soldering is required, and people who don't have any experience with the materials can get good results on the first job. Unfortunately, the building codes in some areas don't allow it for potable-water piping. So be sure to check with your local code authorities before putting it in your house.

Plastic water pipe can also be joined to steel and copper pipe by means of plastic threaded adapters.

Both male and female plastic adapters are available. One end of the plastic adapter is glued to the plastic pipe and the other is threaded into a fitting or onto a pipe. When joining plastic water pipe to existing metal piping, wrap the male threads with plastic pipe-joint sealant tape. Because plastic female adapters can expand when threaded onto male threads, a better choice is to use a plastic male adapter threaded into a copper or steel female adapter or other fitting.

1 Make cuts with plastic pipe-cutting shears

Joining CPVC plastic pipe

With one exception, CPVC plastic water pipe is put together the same way as plastic drainage pipe. Plastic pipe has a shiny residue on its surface that should be either lightly sanded or treated with a solvent primer before the cement is applied. A fine-grit sandpaper works well for the ends of the pipe but is a little harder to use for the

inside of the fittings. Most people opt for a solvent primer instead because it's faster to use and more thorough. Simply brush the surfaces to be joined with the primer, wait a few seconds, and wipe them clean with a soft cloth. Then apply the glue to the pipe and fitting and push them together with a slight twist.

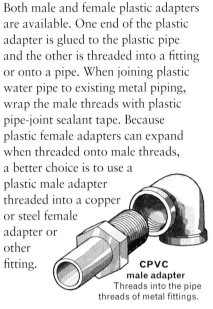

CPVC male adapter
Threads into the pipe threads of metal fittings.

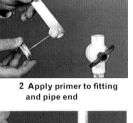

2 Apply primer to fitting and pipe end

Joining PEX to fittings

PEX pipe is the new kid on the block. It's made of polyethylene plastic and is becoming more popular, particularly with DIYers. It usually comes in red, white, or blue colors and is sold in easy-to-handle rolls. It has little coil memory and is not affected by corrosive soil or water. And it's

much more forgiving than copper or CPVC in freezing temperatures. It's usually joined to rigid brass or plastic fittings with simple-to-install clamps. It doesn't have the track record of copper or even CPVC at this point, but it's gaining code acceptance all the time.

3 Test-fit joint and mark final alignment

PEX pipe attaches to fitting with simple clamps

4 Apply cement and push pipe into fitting

Plastic supply-pipe types

Chlorinated polyvinyl chloride (CPVC)

A versatile plastic pipe suitable for both hot and cold supply lines, local codes permitting.

Polybutylene (PB)

An easy-to-install pipe that was popular in the seventies and eighties but is no longer on the market. To make repairs to a PB piping system, install CPVC or copper transition fittings.

Cross–linked polyethylene (PEX)

This pipe is most often used for in-floor radiant heating systems. And it's been used for some time in mobile and modular houses. But it's gaining in popularity for hot-and cold-water supply lines in site-built houses. Generally, it's available only at professional plumbing-supply outlets.

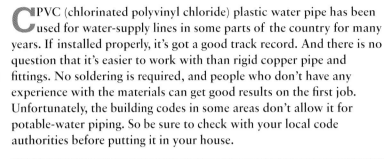

CPVC

PB

PEX

Working with steel pipe

Steel pipe is available in galvanized and black versions. Galvanized pipe is used for water-supply lines and drainage and vent lines, while black steel (often called black iron) is used primarily for gas piping. Though they are put together in exactly the same way, you should avoid mixing the two. When galvanized iron is used on gas installations, the gas in the line can attack the zinc plating and may cause it to flake off. These zinc flakes can be carried through the system and may clog the orifice and control valve of a water heater or furnace. On the other hand, if black pipe is used in water-supply lines, it will rust shut in a matter of months.

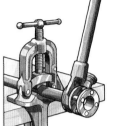

Cutting threads
To cut threads on a steel pipe you need a pipe vise to hold the workpiece and a cutting die mounted in a long cranking handle.

Cutting and threading steel pipe

Steel pipe can be cut with a hacksaw. In fact, when cutting out a section of existing pipe, a hacksaw is your best choice. When you intend to thread the cut end, however, a wheel cutter will give you a much more uniform cut. Wheel cutters can be found at most tool-rental stores along with the threading dies you'll need.

To determine the exact length of pipe, measure between the two fittings and add the depth of the threads inside each fitting for your total length. Then mark the pipe with a crayon. Place the pipe in a pipe vise and tighten the cutter on the pipe so that the wheel is directly on your mark. Then tighten the wheel one-half turn and rotate the cutter around the pipe. When the cutting wheel turns in its groove easily, tighten it another turn and rotate the cutter again. Repeat the process until the pipe is cut completely through.

Once the cut is made, leave the pipe in the vise and get ready to cut new threads. Cover the first inch of the pipe with cutting oil and slide the cylinder of the die onto the pipe. Set the lock on the die to the "cut" position. Then, while pressing the die onto the pipe with the palm of your hand, crank the die handle. When the die teeth begin to cut into the metal, you will feel some resistance. You will then be ready to crank the handle steadily around the pipe to cut the threads.

About every two rounds, stop and pour oil through the die head and onto the new threads. This is very important. Without oil, the pipe will heat up and swell until you can no longer turn the handle. Dry pipe threads will also ruin the die cutters in short order.

Continue cranking and oiling until the first of the new threads shows through the front of the die. Then reverse the direction lock on the handle and spin the die off the pipe. Thread the other end and you're done. All threaded steel joints should be put together with Teflon pipe-joint tape or pipe-joint compound, on the male side only.

Teflon tape
Use this sealing tape on the threads of all steel pipe joints.

Steel pipe fittings

Steel pipe is put together with threaded joints. Because steel was the predominant residential piping material for most of the twentieth century, you will find it in many older homes. You may never need to install steel piping, but chances are you will confront it when making changes and repairs.

Steel pipe comes in 21-foot lengths and is threaded on each end at the factory. It also comes in short precut, prethreaded lengths called nipples that graduate in 1/2-inch increments from 1 inch to approximately 1 foot. When you need custom lengths, you have to cut and thread them yourself, using a die cutter. Some well-equipped, and usually older, hardware stores will do the job for you.

Joining steel pipe and fittings
You need two pipe wrenches to tighten threaded steel joints. One holds pipe, one holds fitting.

Union Male/female adapter Threaded nipple

Coupling Reducer coupling Reducing tee

90° ell Reducing ell Combination tee

Steel fittings
You will find a steel fitting for nearly every piping joint. Here are nine of the most common ones.

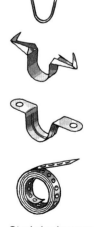

Steel pipe hangers
Like other pipe, steel pipe must be hung from joists every 6 feet with hangers (above, from top): wire hanger, two strap hangers, and perforated strap. examples of wire hangers.

Joining copper pipe

Fire Precautions

Clean fitting with small wire brush

Clean pipe with steel wool or sandpaper

Apply flux to the fitting and the pipe

Heat joint with torch and apply solder

Soldered joints are found in runs of copper pipe. To install them, all you'll need is an inexpensive torch, the correct solder and flux, some abrasive, and a willingness to try.

Applying solder

Because comfort is important when soldering at odd angles, it's a good idea to precut some solder and hold this shorter piece in your hand instead of trying to handle the whole spool. Wind about 2 feet around your hand and leave about 10 inches free. Then pull the loop from your hand and squeeze it into a handle.

If you are right-handed, place the solder in your right hand and the torch in your left. Light the torch and open the valve all the way. Place the torch tip so that the flame hits the hub of the fitting straight on. The tip should be about ¾ inch away from the fitting. If yours is not a turbo tip, heat one side for a few seconds until the flux begins to liquefy, and then move around the fitting and heat the far side while touching the solder to the fitting.

Keep the solder opposite the torch flame and continue to touch the fitting until the solder liquefies and wraps around the fitting quickly. As soon as the fitting is hot enough to pull solder around it, take the heat away and push solder into the fitting.

If the fitting will not take solder easily, pull the solder away and heat the fitting for a few more seconds. Then push the solder in. A ¾-inch fitting should take about ¾ inch of solder. When the hub has taken enough solder, move on to the next hub on that fitting. Always start with the bottom joint on a fitting and work up. When all joints on that fitting are soldered, watch the rim of the last joint carefully. When the fitting starts to cool, it will draw solder into the joint. This cooling draw is your assurance that the joint is a good one. If the solder around the rim of a joint stays puddled and does not draw in when it cools, heat until the solder liquefies, and then wait again for it to draw in slightly. When you are satisfied that the last joint is a good one, wipe the fitting of excess solder and move on to the next fitting. When all fittings have cooled, turn the water on and check each joint periodically for leaks.

Of course, working with a torch requires a few precautionary measures. When soldering a fitting that is next to a floor joist or any combustible surface, you will have to protect that surface. The simplest protection method is to fold a piece of sheet metal over so that it has a double thickness. Then slide this double wall of metal between the fitting and the combustible surface. If you cannot sufficiently protect the area around the fitting, you may wish to solder that section elsewhere and install it already soldered.

To avoid scorching the rubber washers and diaphragms inside valves, always solder them with the handles turned open. This will diffuse enough heat to keep the seals from being ruined. Remember, use only as much heat as is needed to draw the solder evenly around the joint. The most common beginner's mistake is too much heat, not too little.

Torches

Most hardware stores offer small, inexpensive torch kits (about $20) that include a replaceable propane, or MAPP gas, bottle, a regulator valve, and a flame tip. The best of these kits offer a turbo tip that spins the flame as it exits the tip. Turbo tips are useful because they wrap flames around a pipe so that you do not have to heat both sides of a fitting. You can also rent larger propane tanks with hose-mounted tips that hold much more gas.

Flux and solder

The next ingredient you will need is a good self-cleaning flux. The right flux is critical to achieving a leakproof soldering job. Because you will sometimes need to reflux heated fittings, you will want to avoid soldering paste. Choose, instead, a can or jar of self-cleaning flux that has the consistency of butter. The cleaning agents in this flux boil away any chemical residues and tarnish that build up on copper. Also buy several acid brushes so that you can brush additional flux onto a hot fitting without burning yourself.

Choosing the right solder is also important. Until the late eighties, lead in varying amounts was always present in solder used for plumbing systems. It was easy to use and very durable. But it was banned by the EPA because of the health risks of lead leaching into drinking water. Use only lead-free solder on plumbing joints. Resist all urging by salespeople to use acid-core solder for plumbing work.

Fittings for remodeling and repair

Repair and remodeling work often require that you cut a section of pipe from between two fittings. This is easily done with a hacksaw. Once the cut is made, you will need to back each section of remaining pipe out of its fitting. Use two pipe wrenches, one to unthread the pipe and one to hold the fitting so that joints farther down the line won't be disturbed. If other joints are inadvertently turned, you might cause leaks.

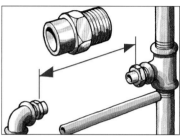

Steel replacement pipes need a union fitting

Reconnecting with copper or plastic pipe

Splicing in new pipe between two existing steel fittings is easier to do with copper or plastic. In both cases, threaded adapters can be screwed into the steel fittings. In the case of copper, the remaining joints between the replacement pipe and the adapters will have to be soldered. In the case of plastic pipes, all the joints will be glued. Because plastic water pipe is not universally accepted for water supply lines, you should check with your local code authorities before installing it for that purpose. Plastic drain and vent lines are accepted everywhere.

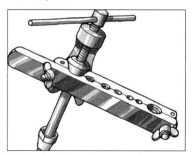

Copper pipe is joined to steel pipe with adapters

Working with copper pipe

Copper pipe is available in four wall-thicknesses. Type K is the thickest and is used primarily for underground water services and under concrete for supply lines. It comes in soft coils.

Type L offers the next thickest pipe wall. It is available in soft coils or rigid sticks. The soft version is typically used in gas pipe installations and is connected with flare fittings.

The thinnest allowable supply-line pipe is type M. It is made only in 20-foot rigid lengths and is the most widely used in residential water systems.

The thinnest-walled copper pipe is DWV. As its initials imply, it is used as drain, waste, and vent piping. Although seldom used now for drainage and vent piping, it was widely used in the fifties.

All copper pipe can be cut with a hacksaw, but if you intend to use flare fittings on soft copper, a wheel cutter will give a more uniform edge. All copper can be soldered, and all soft copper can be flared for use with flare fittings. Copper drainage pipe can be joined to steel, plastic, or cast-iron pipe with no-hub couplings. Hard-copper supply connections can also be joined with compression fittings.

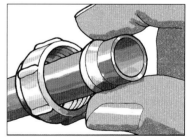

Flaring tool forms flare on end of soft pipe

Flare and compression fittings

As its name implies, a flare fitting requires that you flare the pipe to fit the fitting. Slide the flare nut onto soft copper pipe and clamp the flaring die within ⅛ inch of the end of the pipe. Thread the flaring tool into the pipe end until the end of the pipe expands evenly against the tapered die seat. Remove the tool and draw the fitting together with two wrenches.

A compression fitting operates in reverse fashion and so it does not require a special tool. Simply slide the fitting nut and brass compression ring onto hard or soft copper pipe and thread the nut onto its fitting. Hand-tighten the nut, one to one and a half turns. Use pipe-joint compound on all flare and compression fittings.

Compression joint is made with nut and brass ring

Working with cast-iron pipe

You can cut cast-iron pipe with a chisel by tapping lightly in a line around the pipe until it breaks. But the best way is to use a snap cutter. This is a ratchet-like tool with a chain that wraps around pipe and cutting wheels that clamp onto the pipe. As the tool turns, the wheels cut the pipe. Snap cutters are available at most tool rental outlets.

Traditional hub and spigot joints are now made with neoprene gaskets. Where hubs are not available or where hubless cast iron is joined to plastic, steel, or copper pipe, no-hub couplings make the easiest connection.

Rented snap cutter cuts cast iron

Drain-cleaning techniques

Clearing toilet blockages

Soap, hair, food particles, and cooking grease all help to clog drainage lines. Occasionally a fixture trap will accumulate a blockage that can be forced clear with a plunger or compressed air. Most blockages build up inside pipes over an extended period of time, however, and must be cabled, or "snaked," to be opened. The method you choose will depend upon the fixture involved and the size of the drainage line.

Forcing fixture traps

Plungers and cans of compressed air can both be used to free simple trap clogs. When forcing a clog from a trap with either of these, be sure to plug any connecting airways. When plunging a lavatory, for example, use a wet rag to plug the overflow hole in the basin. When forcing the trap of a two-compartment sink, plug the opposite drain. After the debris has been forced through the trap and into the drain line, run very hot water through the line to move the clog into the main stack or soil pipe.

Snaking fixture drains

Remove trap and put snake into drain pipe

When you wish to clean the drain line of any fixture with a snake, you will first have to remove the trap. Use a pipe wrench or adjustable pliers to loosen the nuts at the top of the trap and at the drain connection near the wall. With S-traps, loosen the nuts near the floor and at the trap. To avoid cracking or breaking a chrome P-trap, hold it firmly and turn the nut with steady, even pressure.

Snaking a shower

If drain water backs up into a tub or shower from another fixture, it probably means that the main sewer line is clogged. If a tub or shower drains slowly, or not at all, then you should snake the tub or shower trap and drain line. To snake a tub, remove the coverplate from the overflow valve and push the cable into the overflow pipe. This is easier than working through the drain opening. Stand-alone showers don't have overflow openings, so they have to be snaked through the drain.

Snaking a sewer line

You can rent a sewer-cleaning machine, but before doing so, get several bids from professional drain-cleaning companies. Often they can do the job for just a little more than the cost of the machine rental. And you can avoid all the aggravation that's involved. Most sewer clogs are either from tree roots or collapsed pipes and both repair jobs are better left to a professional.

Sewer-cleaning machines These tools are aggressive pieces of equipment that can clear out serious blockages.

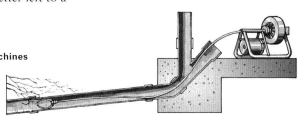

Occasionally a toilet will clog and overflow. Most toilets clog at the top of the trap because that is where the trap is the smallest. Toothpaste caps, hairpins, and combs are regular culprits.

Start by trying to plunge the toilet trap. A plunger with a collapsible funnel works best. If plunging doesn't do the trick, remove the water from the bowl and use a small mirror and a flashlight to look up into the trap. If you can see the obstruction, chances are you can reach it with a wire hook.

If all else fails, rent a closet auger and crank the auger through the trap several times. The auger's cable is just long enough to reach the toilet flange. As you pull the cable out of the trap, keep cranking the handle.

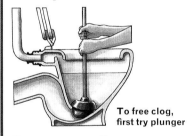

To free clog, first try plunger

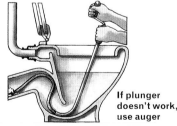

If plunger doesn't work, use auger

Faucet replacement

Faucet installation has not changed much over the years. While plastic fasteners and flexible supply risers have made the job easier, the process remains much the same. Often the most complicated part of the job is selecting the faucet itself. One faucet-buying trip to a plumbing supply showroom, to say nothing of visiting the average home-center megastore, can set your head spinning. The number of different models and the jargon (single-handle, double-handle, compression, cartridge, ceramic cartridge, retro, modern) can be overwhelming. Start by matching your existing faucet design. By doing this you'll know at least one model that will work for you.

Removing a faucet

The most troublesome part of replacing a faucet is getting the old faucet off. Start by shutting off the faucet's water supply, either at the meter or at a shutoff valve located under the sink. Turn the faucet on to relieve the pressure. Then loosen the nuts that connect the riser pipes to the supply lines and the faucet. A basin wrench will help you reach the coupling nuts high up under the sink. When these nuts are loose, bend the risers slightly so that they can be pulled out of the faucet and supply fittings.

Next, use a basin wrench to undo the nuts that hold the faucet to the sink. If the faucet is old and the nuts corroded, first spray penetrating oil on the threads. If this does not help loosen the nuts, use a small cold chisel and hammer and gently tap the nuts in a counterclockwise direction to break them loose. Once they are broken loose, back off the nuts with a basin wrench.

In a few cases, even these methods will not free the fastening nuts. If this happens to you, your only recourse is to saw through the nut with a hacksaw blade.

Some faucet styles mount from the bottom and are held to the sink or countertop by a locknut under the handle escutcheon. To remove a bottom-mounted faucet, first remove the handles, then the escutcheons. Escutcheons are usually screwed on and can be removed by threading them counterclockwise. Under the escutcheon, you will find the locknuts. Undo these nuts and the faucet should fall out.

Because years of soap and mineral buildup can leave a ridge around the edge of the faucet plate, you may have to clean the faucet area of the sink before installing a new faucet. A fifty-fifty mixture of white vinegar and warm water used in conjunction with a single-edged razor blade will help you remove this ridge. Just soak the buildup and scrape it away.

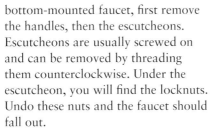

NUT · BASIN WRENCH · SUPPLY · SHUTOFF

Installing a new faucet

After you've cleaned the sink, set the new faucet in place with the rubber or plastic spacer between the faucet and sink. Then reach under the sink and thread the new washers and nuts onto the faucet until the nuts are fingertight. Before tightening the faucet nuts, however, go back and straighten the faucet so that the back of the coverplate is parallel with the back edge of the sink. When the faucet is straight, tighten the nuts.

When the faucet is fastened in place, you will be ready to reconnect the supply risers. It is usually a good idea to start with new risers. Different types are available. Soft copper risers are okay if they aren't visible, in places like under a kitchen sink or bathroom vanity. But where the risers do show, chrome-plated copper is a better choice, as are stainless-steel flexible risers. Both include a bulb-shaped head that fits into the ground joint surface of the faucet's hot- and cold-water inlets. The riser nuts slide onto the pipe from the other end. When you tighten these nuts to the faucets, the bulb-shaped head is pressed into the ground joints and makes a watertight seal. The supply-line ends of the risers are connected to shutoff valves with compression fittings.

Remove old faucet and lower new one in place

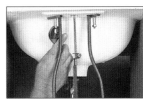

Tighten nuts from below to hold faucet

Attach supply risers to shutoff valves

WASHER · PERFORATED DISC · SCREEN · BODY

Cleaning aerators
Most kitchen faucets have aerators that can clog. To clean them, unthread the body and wash the screen, disk, and washer.

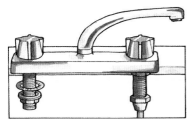

Top-mount faucet
This is installed from above and is held in place with a locknut and washer from below.

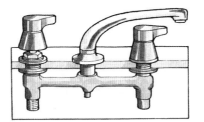

Bottom-mount faucet
This is installed from below and is held in place with a locknut and washer from above.

Faucet repairs

Faucet repair is as simple or as complex as the design of the faucet involved. In general terms, there are four basic faucet mechanisms in use today. The oldest type, still found in many faucets and in most valves, uses the stem-and-seat principle. More recent designs feature replaceable cores, rotating balls, and ceramic disks. With each of these types, the internal mechanism turns or rotates until holes in the mechanism align with holes in the faucet, allowing water to pass through. The degree of alignment determines the mixture of hot and cold water. In each case, repair is relatively simple and inexpensive. Only when a faucet body itself is defective is faucet replacement absolutely necessary.

Typical stem-and-seat faucet

1 Index cap
2 Handle screw
3 Handle
4 Locknut
5 Stem
6 Stem threads
7 O-ring
8 Seat washer
9 Washer screw
10 Faucet body

Heatproof grease
Before reassembling a faucet, cover all moving parts with heatproof grease, which won't dissolve in hot water. It greatly increases the life of replacement parts and makes the faucet much easier to take apart the next time service is needed. Remember to grease the handle sockets as well.

Repairing stem-and-seat faucets

To repair stem-and-seat faucets, start by removing the handles. Most handles have decorative coverplates (also called index caps) under which are handle screws. Pry off the caps and remove the screws. If a handle has not been removed recently, it may be stuck to the stem. Gently pry up under both sides of the handle with two screwdrivers to free the handle. If the handle will still not loosen, you may need to buy an inexpensive handle puller from your local hardware dealer.

On better faucets, all external parts are made of chrome-plated brass, and these faucets usually come apart easily. Cheaper models feature chrome-plated pot metal, which corrodes easily, making the handles hard to remove. If you damage a pot-metal handle, your best bet is to replace it with a universal-fit replacement handle.

When you have the handle off, undo the escutcheon (if necessary) to get to the locknut. Loosen the locknut with an adjustable wrench. If the locknut backs out several rounds and then stops, turn the stem in or out, depending on the brand, to free the locknut. When the locknut is loose, back the stem out of the faucet. To remove most stems, turn the nut counterclockwise.

On the end of the stem you will find a rubber washer secured by a brass screw or nut. Undo this screw or nut and find a replacement washer that fits the rim of the stem. A tight fit is important here. The washer should not be too big or too small. Press the washer into the seat and install the screw or nut. Because brass screws can become brittle with age, it's a good idea to

replace the screw when you replace a washer. If you are uncertain about which washer to use, take the stem to a well-stocked hardware store and ask the clerk to pick out the right one for you.

Remove nut or screw

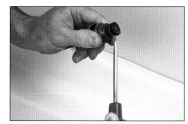

Pry washer off stem

Dealing with seat damage

When a defective washer is allowed to leak for an extended period of time, the pressure of the water will cut a channel in the faucet seat. For this reason, always repair a leaking faucet immediately. A defective seat will chew up new washers in short order, so always check the seat when you replace a washer.

If you find a channel in the seat, replace the seat. A seat wrench will allow you to unscrew a removable seat from a faucet

body. Some seats are machined into the brass body of a faucet and therefore cannot be removed. If your faucet seats are pitted and cannot be replaced, your only alternative is to grind the entire seat rim to a level below the surface of the pit. While this may sound difficult, it is not. You can buy an inexpensive seat grinder from your local hardware store, and once the faucet is apart, you can do the job in a matter of minutes.

Remove seat with seat wrench

Regrind seat with grinder tool

Seat-and-spring faucet repairs

Seat-and-spring type faucets, one of a variety that are known as washerless faucets, have become quite popular in recent years, both because of their durability and because they are easy to repair. The operating mechanism of a seat-and-spring faucet consists of a stainless-steel or plastic ball that is turned and aligned with water openings in the faucet body as the single handle is manipulated. The openings in the faucet body contain spring-loaded rubber caps, or seats, which press against the ball and prevent leaking when in the off position. When this type of faucet drips, it is because these rubber caps and springs are worn.

Repair kits for seat-and-spring faucets are inexpensive and come with everything needed to completely rebuild a faucet. It is important to identify the faucet by brand name when asking for a repair kit in order to get the correct parts. The common brand names are Delta and Peerless. Kits come with complete instructions. The repairs you make will depend upon the location and nature of the leak.

Repairing handle leaks

If your seat-and-spring faucet leaks around the handle but does not drip from the spout, just tighten the faucet cap. The cap is the threaded dome that holds the mechanism in place. The repair kit comes with a small cap wrench, or you can use slip-joint pliers to tighten a cap. You simply remove the handle with an Allen wrench, then turn the cap clockwise until the leak stops. Do not overtighten. Pliers can sometimes scratch the chrome. For added protection, wrap the jaws with a soft cloth.

Replacing seats and springs

If the faucet drips, you must take the faucet apart. This is easily done by using the proprietary cap wrench. Use the Allen wrench side of the tool to loosen the handle set screw. Pull the handle off. Then use the cap wrench to loosen and remove the cap. Under the cap you will find a nylon and rubber cam covering a stainless-steel ball. Remove the cam assembly and pull the ball up and out of the faucet body. Inside the faucet you will see two or three hollow rubber caps, or seats, mounted on two small springs.

Insert a needle-nose pliers into the faucet body and pull the seats and springs out. Discard the worn seats and springs. Then slide the new springs and seats into the faucet holes. When the spring-loaded seats are in place, reinstall the ball-and-cam assembly.

The kit comes with a new cam seal that should be installed before putting the cam in place. The cam assembly will have a tab on one side that corresponds with a slot in the faucet. Match the tab with the slot and press the cam assembly in place over the ball. Tighten the cap and replace the handle.

If your seat-and-spring faucet also leaks around the spout collar, replace the collar O-rings before putting the cap and handle back on. To replace collar O-rings, pull up evenly and firmly on the spout until it comes free. Use a knife to cut the old O-rings from the slots and slide the new rings over the body until they fit into the O-ring slots. Apply heat-proof grease to the rings and press the spout collar back on, rotating it gently as you go. Complete the job by reinstalling the cap and handle.

Seat-and-spring faucets

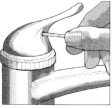

Allen wrench removes handle

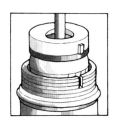

Pliers tighten faucet cap

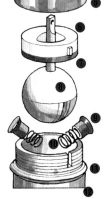

Typical seat-and-spring faucet

1 Handle
2 Set screw
3 Cap
4 Spout
5 Spout collar
6 Cam collar
7 Cam seal
8 Ball
9 Spring cap
10 Spring
11 O-ring
12 Faucet body

To remove the cam and ball, simply pull them out of the faucet body.

Remove the springs and cap seals with a pair of needle-nose pliers.

To replace ball, line up the tab in the ball with the slot in the faucet.

Faucet repairs

Repairing cartridge-type single-handle faucets

Typical single-handle cartridge faucet

1 Cap
2 Handle
3 Spout
4 Retainer nut
5 Cartridge stem
6 Retainer clip
7 O-ring
8 Faucet body

Cartridge-type washerless faucets have enjoyed wide popular use because of their simplicity and durability. They are available in single-handle and two-handle versions. Unlike the single-handle seat-and-spring mechanism, the cartridge type has a core instead of a ball. This type of faucet is marketed widely under the Moen trade name.

All single-handle Moen faucets use the same core mechanism, but other aspects vary with price. In terms of repair, the only notable difference is in the way the handle covers come off.

If your Moen single-handle faucet has a flat chrome coverplate with the trade name pressed into it, you must first pry the coverplate up with a knife to get to the handle screw. Other models have a plastic hood that covers the handle screw and top of the faucet. These hoods simply pull up and off.

Below the handle you will find the cartridge stem. If yours is a chrome coverplate model, you will also need to remove a retainer nut. Just below the stem, or pivot nut, you will see a brass clip inserted into the side of the cartridge stem. This clip locks the cartridge in place. After you have turned off the water, pull the clip out with pliers. When the clip is removed, you will be able to pull the cartridge out of the faucet body.

Press the new cartridge in place, making sure that it's aligned the same way as the one you took out. Seat the cartridge by pressing it down until the cartridge is in far enough to accept the clip and you can slide the clip into place. Then replace the retainer nut, spout, and handle. Make sure that the handle slips into the groove in the retainer nut before replacing the screw. The handle works properly when it lifts and lowers the stem smoothly.

Remove handle screw and handle

Remove retainer clip with needlenose pliers

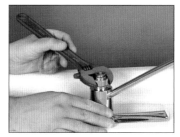
Remove cartridge retainer nut

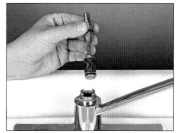
Pull old cartridge straight up and out

Repairing washerless two-handle faucets

Washerless faucets are also available in two-handle designs. The repair kit includes a cartridge and a seat assembly.

To make the repair, start by prying off the index cap and removing the handle screw. When the handle is off, remove the locknut that holds the cartridge in place. Then pull the old cartridge up and out of the faucet. Replace the seat and spring as you would with a single-handle faucet.

The new cartridge must be properly aligned before it can be installed. On the side of each cartridge you will see a tab, called a key. And on the faucet body side you will see a slot, called a keyway. Also note a stop at the top of the cartridge (see above). Align the key so that it is directly over the keyway. Then insert the cartridge so the stop is facing the spout. Replace and tighten the locknut until it is snug. Press the handle onto the new stem and replace the handle screw and index cap.

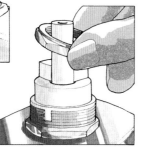
Remove locknut and cartridge

Replace seat assemblies

Repairing ceramic-disk faucets

When a ceramic-disk faucet leaks, the leakage is likely to show up around the base of the faucet. Getting to the operational part of these faucets is different than in other models. Instead of prying off the index cap to remove the handle, you must tip the handle back to reveal a set screw under the front of the handle. Use an Allen wrench to loosen the screw. But having the handle removed still does not give you access to the internal mechanism. You must also remove the chrome faucet cover. With older models, you will need to loosen the pop-up drain lever and undo two brass screws from the underside of the faucet. Newer models have a slot screw in the handle and a brass keeper ring that allows you to remove the cover from above.

When the faucet cover is off, you will find a ceramic disk secured by two brass bolts to the base of the faucet. Undo these bolts and the disk

should lift off. Take this disk with you to your plumbing-supply store and buy an identical replacement disk.

To install the new disk, align the ports of the disk with those of the faucet base. Make sure that the flange under the cartridge bolt holes fits into the rim around the bolt holes in the body plate. When all is perfectly aligned, replace the disk bolts and refasten the faucet cover and handle. Turn on the water and test for leaks.

Remove handle set screw with Allen wrench

Remove faucet cover to reach ceramic disk

Unscrew bolts and remove ceramic disk

Slide new disk into faucet and screw in place

Repairing two-handle cartridge-type faucets

Some two-handle faucets also use cartridges for their internal mechanisms. To remove a defective two-handle cartridge, start by removing the index cap with a knife. Then remove the handle screw and handle. Under the handle is a large nut that holds the cartridge in place. Undo this nut with pliers. Then lift the cartridge out by the stem.

To install a new cartridge, turn the cartridge stem in a counterclockwise direction so that the holes of the cartridge are aligned. Then push the cartridge straight down into the faucet, making sure that the key at the top of the cartridge fits into the

slot in the faucet. When you've seated the cartridge, screw the cartridge nut back on and tighten with pliers until snug. Then replace the handle, handle screw, and index cap.

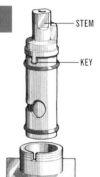
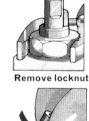

STEM
KEY

Remove locknut

Two-handle cartridge

Turn to align cartridge

Sillcock repair

A sillcock is a stem-and-seat faucet with a long stem. To repair one, shut off the water at the meter or shut-off valve. Then loosen the locknut that holds the stem and pull the stem out. If it is stubborn, twist and pull it out with locking pliers. Replace the washer, apply heatproof grease, and replace the stem.

Sillcocks often wear out faster than ordinary faucets due to a common mistake: Because water continues to drain from the spout for a few seconds after the valve is shut, many people think the valve is starting to leak, so continue to turn the handle. This extra pressure ruins stem washers in a hurry.

Replacing freezeless sillcocks

Freezeless sillcocks differ from ordinary outside faucets in that they can be left on during freezing weather. Instead of stopping the water outside the home, they stop water inside by means of a long faucet stem. The only way a freezeless sillcock can freeze is if a hose is left connected in cold weather or if it has been installed without sufficient pitch to drain. When either situation occurs, sillcocks will freeze and split just inside the home near the valve seat.

To replace a sillcock, turn off the water and unthread the sillcock from the pipe in the basement. Buy a new one the same length and thread it back into the supply line.

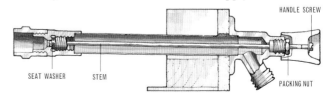

HANDLE SCREW
SEAT WASHER   STEM
PACKING NUT

Replacing lavatories

Replacing a wall-hung lavatory with a pedestal sink or a vanity cabinet and countertop basin can have a big design impact on a small room. Add some fresh paint, new light fixtures, maybe some new flooring, and a new mirror or medicine cabinet and you'll completely change the room.

Measuring and planning

Start by measuring the space around the existing lavatory to determine what size cabinet your bathroom will allow. Because storage space is always scarce, try for the biggest vanity that will fit in your space. Factory-made models come in standard sizes to fit many opening widths and depths; most cabinet stores have a huge variety of material and finish choices available. You'll also be able to choose what combination of doors and drawers the cabinet will have.

Countertops and lavatory basins are other major considerations. For standard-size cabinets, cultured-marble tops with basins molded into them are economical choices. Other options are plastic laminate countertops with china, cast-iron, or enameled-steel basins. Solid surface tops with integral basins and natural stone tops with undermount sinks occupy the high end.

Removing a wall-hung lavatory

To remove a wall-hung lav, start by disconnecting the trap and water-supply risers. If your lav does not have shutoff valves between the risers and supply lines, now might be a good time to install them. With valves on both supply lines, you will not have to shut down the entire water system when working on just one fixture.

Once the piping is disconnected, check to see if the back of the lavatory is secured to the wall by anchor screws. These screws will be located at the back of the lav just under the apron. If anchor screws are present, remove them. Then grab the lav by its sides and pull up. It should lift right off the mounting bracket. Remove the mounting bracket by undoing the screws that fasten it to the wall. Before installing the new vanity, check to see if the wall above the vanity needs

to be repaired or painted. Sometimes the screw holes from the mounting bracket will show above the new vanity. Filling these holes and other cosmetic repairs may be necessary before the vanity can be set in place.

With the opening ready, slide the new vanity in place and secure it to the wall with long screws driven through the back of cabinet and into the studs inside the wall. In some cases you may have to cut openings in the vanity for the drainpipe and supply lines. Once the cabinet is in place, you are ready to install the countertop. In the case of a cultured-marble top, simply set it on the vanity and glue it to the cabinet top with construction adhesive. In the case of a factory- or custom-made countertop, screw the top to the corner brackets of the vanity from inside the cabinet.

Cutting a basin opening

Some lav basins come with a paper template for marking the correct cutline on the countertop. But if yours didn't, you can simply turn over the sink on the countertop and trace around its perimeter. Then measure the width of the basin lip and draw a second line inside the first to allow for the lip. Bore an access hole on the waste side of the cut line for the blade of a sabre saw. Cut

the opening. To avoid chipping the countertop, use a fine-tooth blade and advance the saw with steady, even pressure.

Because it is much easier to install a faucet and pop-up assembly from above, attach the faucet and the pop-up now. Then turn over the basin, put it in the opening, and attach it to the countertop. Caulk around the rim.

To install a lavatory faucet, insert the faucet supply shanks through the basin faucet holes. Then slide the large spacing washer onto the shanks from below and tighten the locknut on each shank. Make sure that the faucet is centered before tightening the locknuts.

To install a pop-up drain assembly, pack putty around the drain flange and thread the pop-up waste pipe into the basin gasket until the flange is seated in the drain opening. Follow by threading the tailpiece into the pop-up waste pipe.

To connect the pop-up mechanism, insert the lift rod into the opening at the back of the faucet. Then slide one end of the adjustment strip onto the lift rod and the other onto the pop-up lever. Finally, pull the pop-up lever all they way down and tighten the adjustment screw.

When the basin is in place and hooked up to its trap and water supplies, use water-soluble latex caulk to seal the basin to the counter. Wet the areas to be caulked first. Then apply a bead of caulk around the faucet base. Push caulk into the cracks. Then wipe all excess caulk away with a damp cloth.

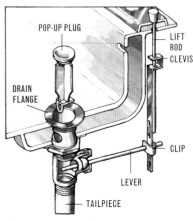

Typical pop-up drain assembly

Replacing a kitchen sink

Replacing a kitchen sink is not a difficult task. But how you proceed depends on the sink you choose and whether you'll be replacing the countertop or keeping the old one.

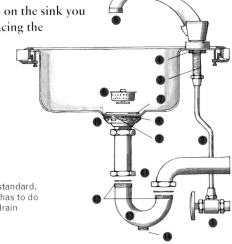

Typical sink installation details

1 Shutoff valve	8 Rubber washer
2 Supply tube	9 Paper washer
3 Pipe threads	10 Spud nut
4 Lock nut	11 Slip nut
5 Aerator	12 Rubber washer
6 Strainer	13 P-trap
7 Putty	14 Cleanout plug

The components of a kitchen sink are fairly standard, no matter what model you choose. The sink has to do three things without leaking: receive water, drain waste, and stay attached to the countertop.

There are plenty of design choices when it comes to home kitchen sinks, faucets, and accessories. Material and finish options are also daunting. Here's a sampling of the options you'll see at your local home center or kitchen-and-bath-supply outlets.

Double sink with left-hand drainboard

Single sink with right-hand drainboard

Double sink with cutting-board insert

Sink with disposer bowl and cutting-board insert

Sink with sink rim

Self-rimming sink edge

Mounting a stainless-steel sink

Stainless-steel sinks are available in a wide range of prices. The more shiny the surface, the more expensive the sink. Stainless-steel sinks do not require sink rims to hold them in place. Instead, the rim of the sink rests on the top of the counter and is held against the countertop by fastening clips from the underside of the counter. Stainless-steel sinks will usually fit the same opening as a sink-rim type and therefore make good replacements. Measure before you buy.

Removing the old sink

If you plan to replace your old countertop, there is probably no need to pull the sink from it. Simply disconnect the trap, disposer, and water supplies, remove the screws from the underside of the countertop, and pull the sink and countertop up together. If you wish to save the basket strainers, disposer flange, or faucet, these are much easier to remove when the countertop is off the cabinets.

If you plan to save the countertop and replace only the sink, start by disconnecting the water supplies, trap, and disposer. Then loosen the clips around the underside of the sink rim,

using a screwdriver or socket wrench. Carefully slide a putty knife under the sink rim to break the seal of any caulk that's present.

Lift the sink straight up by placing one hand around the faucet base and the other through the disposer opening. With the sink out, you will likely need to clean mineral, putty, and soap buildup from the countertop where the old sink rim rested. A putty knife and household cleanser work well for this job. Just be careful. Both the cleanser and the putty knife can easily scratch the surface of the countertop.

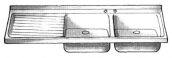

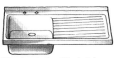

Swivel faucet

High faucet

Self-rimming stainless-steel sink attachment

Replacement sinks

The replacement sink you choose will have one of three possible rims. If you select an enameled cast-iron sink, for example, you will be able to pick between a "self-rimming" model and one that requires a sink rim to fasten it to the countertop.

The self-rimming type has a rolled edge that rests on top of the counter and is caulked in place. The edge of this sink is raised above the counter. The disadvantage of a self-rimming sink is that when wiping the counter,

you cannot simply push spills and food particles into the sink.

As a result, some people prefer a sink that fits flush with the countertop. For a flush fit, choose a sink that uses a rim to suspend it in the counter opening. Sink rims are common on porcelain-steel sinks.

A third rim type is found on stainless-steel sinks. No separate rim is needed but rim clamps are required to fasten the sink to the countertop.

Wire basket

Spray hose

Cutting boards

Strainer and disposals

The chrome trim parts you see in the drains of your sink are not part of the sink basin. They are merely the most visible parts of your disposer and basket strainer. As such, they can be replaced when cosmetic or mechanical problems arise. The job is involved but not difficult and requires only a few tools.

Replacing a basket strainer

Loosen locknut
with a spud wrench

Put putty on new
basket flange

To remove a basket strainer, disconnect the drainpipe from the basket drain threads. Then use a spud wrench or large adjustable pliers to loosen the locknut. To keep the strainer body from turning when you loosen this nut, insert the handles of small pliers into the drain crosspiece from the top. While you turn the nut from below, have someone hold the pliers from above.

If the nut is corroded on the strainer body, you may need to use a small chisel and a hammer to break it loose. If the hammer and chisel do not loosen it, use a hacksaw blade to cut the locknut. Cover one end of the blade with tape to create a handle. Cut across the nut in an upward diagonal motion.

When the locknut is loose, push the strainer body up through the drain opening. Clean the brittle old putty from the flange recess on the sink opening. Then roll new putty out between the palms of your hands so that it forms a soft rope about ½ inch in diameter. Press this putty around the flange of your new strainer and press the strainer in place.

Then slide the rubber washer onto the spud from below. Next, slide the fiber (or paper) washer on, followed by the new locknut. Tighten the locknut until it no longer turns or until the strainer body also begins to turn. From above, clear the excess putty from the rim of the strainer and tighten the locknut again.

Installing a disposer in an existing sink

Loosen locknut with
a spud wrench

Put putty on new
basket flange

Loosen locknut with
a spud wrench

Put putty on new
basket flange

A disposer can be installed in any sink that has a full-size opening. A single-bowl sink is a little less work than a double-bowl sink. But neither is very difficult. All you will need is a disposer, a disposer waste kit, and access to electricity.

To install a disposer in an existing single-bowl sink just remove the waste line, trap, and sink-flange locknut from below and the sink strainer and flange from above. Clean any putty residue from the recessed sink flange. For a double-bowl sink, do the same thing but first remove the waste connector that joins the two drains to the P-trap.

With everything removed, you are ready to install the disposer drain flange. Press putty around the sink flange and press it into the recessed sink opening. Then slide the rubber gasket, fiber gasket, mounting ring, and mounting plate onto the flange from below. While holding everything in place, snap the retaining ring over the ridge on the sink flange. Tighten the screws on the mounting plate until nearly all putty is forced from between the sink and flange, then trim the putty.

With the flange mounted in the sink opening, attach the disposer. Just hold the disposer up to the mounting plate and turn it until the tabs on the top of the disposer seat in the ridges located on the mounting plate.

Some disposers fasten directly to the flange, without need of the mounting ring-and-plate assembly, using a stainless-steel band instead. A rubber collar on the top of the disposer simply slides over the sink flange. Then the stainless-steel band is tightened in place with a nut driver or a screwdriver.

Once the disposer is installed, attach the waste lines and complete the electrical hookups as shown on the facing page.

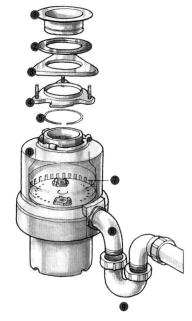

**Disposer
components**

Here are the typical parts needed to install most disposers in a kitchen sink.

1 Sink flange
2 Gasket
3 Mounting ring
4 Mounting plate
5 Snap ring
6 Unit housing
7 Cutters
8 Drain pipe
9 Trap

Most disposers on the market today come with a discharge tube that connects directly to the P-trap under your sink. These tubes work only if you are installing a disposer in a single-bowl sink or if you are replacing a disposer that was previously hooked up to its own trap. Otherwise, you'll need to install a waste kit.

Waste-line connections

When connecting a disposer under a double-bowl sink, both compartments can be drained through a single trap. To make this connection, do not use the discharge tube that came with the disposer. Instead, buy a disposer waste kit. This kit consists of a tee, a tailpiece with a gasket, and a flange. Install the tee vertically between the P-trap and the tailpiece extension from the other sink. The center of the tee branch opening should be only slightly lower than the discharge opening on the disposer.

With the tee installed at the proper height, slip the rubber gasket onto the rim end of the tailpiece and hold it between the disposer opening and the tee opening. The tailpiece will be longer than needed, so you will have to cut to fit. Mark the proper length on the tailpiece. Remember to include the depth of the tee hub in your measurement.

Next, slide the metal flange onto the tailpiece followed by the compression nut and compression ring. Insert the compression end of the tailpiece into the hub on the tee. Push the other end of the tailpiece into the disposer opening. Bolt the flange to the disposer and tighten the compression nut to the tee.

To keep cooking grease from clinging to the sidewalls of the disposer and drain, always run cold water through your disposer when the motor is on. Cold water causes grease to coagulate and flow through the pipes. Hot water thins grease and allows it to build up in pipes.

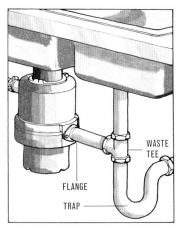
Typical disposer installation

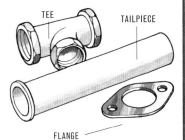
Components of a waste kit

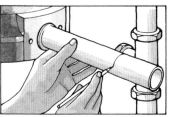
Mark and cut tailpiece

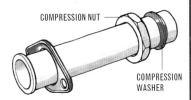
Waste flange tailpiece

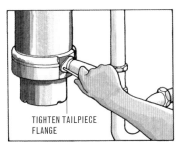
Fasten the flange screws

If you are installing a disposer in a sink that has not had a disposer before, you will have to find some way to get electricity to the disposer and to a switch near the sink. If the basement ceiling beneath your sink is not finished, the easiest alternative is to run a separate cable from your service panel to a wall-mounted switch and then to your disposer. To meet code requirements, however, any cable that's inside the cabinet must be encased in flexible conduit.

If you don't like this option, consider converting an existing receptacle box above your counter into a switch box, if local code allows it. Just fish a short length of wire into the cabinet and over to the disposer.

Once inside the cabinet, the electrical hookup is simple. Remove the coverplate from the bottom of the disposer and pull out the white and black wires. Then, using plastic wire connectors, join the two insulated wires from the switch box to the insulated wires in the disposer. Connect black to black and white to white. Then fasten the uninsulated ground wire from the switch cable to the grounding screw located inside the disposer. Replace the coverplate and test the disposer.

If you are not comfortable making electrical repairs like this, consider hiring an electrician.

Servicing your disposer
Disposers work very well on most foods but have real problems with anything hard or stringy. When the motor pulls against too much resistance, a safety breaker built into the disposer will trip, cutting the power to the motor. To get a stopped disposer started again, first dislodge the motor blades from the blockage. To do this, use the wrench that came with the disposer to reverse the motor manually. The wrench should fit into a key slot on the bottom side of the disposer. Turn the motor back and forth until it spins easily in both directions. Next, find the reset button on the underside of the disposer and press it. Finally, run cold water through the disposer drain and turn on the disposer. This wrench and reset procedure will free most blockages. If the disposer stops again, repeat the procedure.

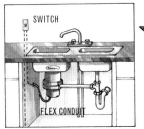
Standard electrical hookup

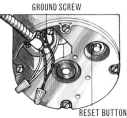
Bottom view of disposer

Toilet installation

There are several reasons why you might remove a toilet. If you want to install a new one, of course, you'll first have to remove the old. You might need to repair part of the bathroom floor or replace a broken toilet flange. Or you might want to install new flooring in the whole room and therefore need to take out the toilet and reset it afterward.

Removing a toilet

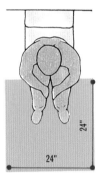

While toilets are heavy and unwieldy, they are also fragile. To complicate the matter, old brass bolts and working parts become brittle with age and fall apart easily. If you wish only to remove a toilet in order to lay flooring, don't separate the tank from the bowl. While the unit will be heavier to move, you will avoid the possibility of damaging tank bolts and spud gasket seals.

Start by shutting off the water at the supply valve. Flush the toilet and sponge the remaining water out of the tank. When the tank is dry, use a paper cup to dip the remaining water out of the bowl. Then undo the water supply at the valve.

Next, pry the bolt caps from the base of the toilet. Under these caps you will find the closet bolts. Older models may have four bolts instead of the two bolts found on more modern stools. The front two bolts will be lag-bolts with removable nuts and the back two will be standard closet bolts mounted through the toilet flange. Use a small adjustable wrench to remove the nuts.

With the closet nuts loose and the supply pipe disconnected, rock the bowl slightly in each direction to break it free from the floor and bowl gasket. Then grab the toilet by the bowl rim just in front of the tank and lift up. Because the bowl gasket will be sticky and dirty, have a newspaper ready to set the toilet on. Then use a putty knife to scrape the remaining wax or putty from the toilet and flange. Discard the old closet bolts.

Turn off the valve and remove riser pipe

Remove caps, then nuts, on closet bolts

Rock toilet from side to side, then lift

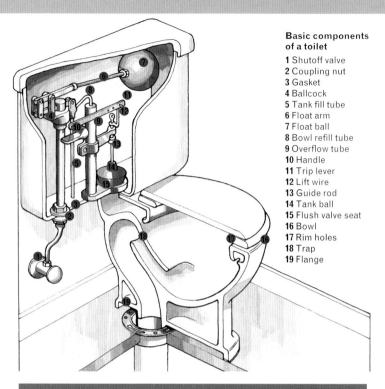

Basic components of a toilet

1 Shutoff valve
2 Coupling nut
3 Gasket
4 Ballcock
5 Tank fill tube
6 Float arm
7 Float ball
8 Bowl refill tube
9 Overflow tube
10 Handle
11 Trip lever
12 Lift wire
13 Guide rod
14 Tank ball
15 Flush valve seat
16 Bowl
17 Rim holes
18 Trap
19 Flange

Resetting a toilet

Before resetting a toilet, you will need to buy a new bowl gasket (usually called a wax ring) and two new closet bolts. Begin by sliding the new closet bolts into the slots in the closet flange and center them so that each is the same distance away from the back wall. Then press the wax ring down on the flange.

Lift the toilet by the bowl rim near the tank and carry it over to the flange. Carefully align the holes in the bowl with the bolts and slowly set the stool down. Press down evenly with all your weight. Then slide the washers and nuts onto the bolts and tighten the nuts slowly, working from one bolt to another. When the base meets the floor and the nuts on the closet bolts seem snug, try rocking the bowl a little. If it moves, tighten the closet nuts

another round. If the bowl does not move, stop. Both flanges and toilet bowls can break if you overtighten the bolts. Retighten after a few days if needed.

Remove old wax ring with putty knife

Slide bolts into flange, then add new wax ring

Making the water connection

Bringing water to the tank

If you are resetting a toilet that you've recently taken up, chances are you will be able to use the original supply riser. First, apply pipe-joint compound to the compression ferrule. Then insert the compression end of the riser into the shutoff valve and slide the other end into the ballcock fitting. If necessary, bend the riser slightly to gain the clearance you need. When both ends are in place, straighten the pipe and tighten the nuts.

If you added a new layer of flooring, you can't use the original supply riser. Installing a new one will be easier anyway, thanks to improved materials and designs.

While standard chrome-plated copper supply risers are bendable, they kink very easily and, once this happens, can't be used. To avoid this problem, choose chrome-plated supplies that are ribbed. These are very flexible and almost impossible to kink.

Also on the market are plastic supply tubes encased in stainless-steel mesh. The plastic makes this tubing flexible and the steel mesh makes it durable. Sink risers are also available in stainless-steel-wrapped plastic.

No matter which type of supply riser you choose, the end that connects to the ballcock will be shaped to accept a flat washer or a cone washer. The other end is designed to accept the compression nut and ferrule from the shutoff valve.

If your supply riser must be cut to length, hold it against the ballcock threads and estimate how much you will have to bend it to make it meet the stool

valve. Then make the two bends as near to the ballcock end of the tube as possible. To avoid kinking the tube, apply steady, even pressure at several points along the length.

Hold the riser in place again and mark where the cut should be made. Be sure to add the depth of the valve socket to the length of the pipe. Use a tubing cutter to make the cut. Then slide the ballcock nut on the pipe from the bottom end, followed by the compression nut and ferrule. Fit the compression end into the shutoff valve socket and push the other end against the ballcock. Tighten the compression nut one full turn after you feel resistance. To tighten the ballcock nut, reach into the tank and hold the ballcock to keep it from spinning.

If you use flexible risers, you won't have to cut anything. Just measure the distance from the shutoff valve to the ballcock and buy a riser that's just a little longer than this measurement.

Next, turn on the water slowly at the shutoff valve and check for leaks. If you find water dripping at either joint just tighten the nut slightly until it stops.

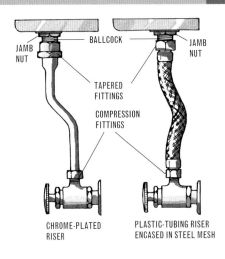

JAMB NUT — BALLCOCK — JAMB NUT

TAPERED FITTINGS

COMPRESSION FITTINGS

CHROME-PLATED RISER

PLASTIC-TUBING RISER ENCASED IN STEEL MESH

Bending pipe

A bending spring is the cheapest and easiest tool for making bends in small-diameter copper pipes. The spring is made of hardened steel and is designed to support the walls of the pipe while it's being bent. This prevents the pipe from kinking. Some bending springs are made to fit inside the pipe, others are meant to slide over the pipe.

To bend small copper pipes like supply risers, slide a spring over the outside of the pipe so it supports the area you want to bend. Hold the tube against your knee and bend it to the required angle. The bent tube might grip the spring, depending on how tight the bend is. If this happens just pull the spring off with a pair of pliers.

Bending springs

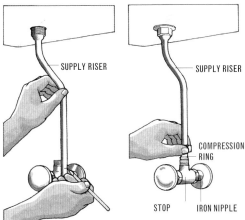

SUPPLY RISER

SUPPLY RISER

COMPRESSION RING

STOP   IRON NIPPLE

Hold riser in place, mark length, and cut

Connect riser to valve with compression fitting

Slide pipe into spring and slowly bend

Installing a new toilet

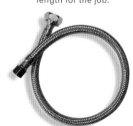

Y our new toilet will come in two boxes. One will contain the bowl and the other the tank. You will have to install the bowl first, but open both boxes. Inside the tank box, you will find closet-bolt caps and retainers that are needed to install the bowl.

Fitting the toilet

Begin by inserting new closet bolts in the slots of the toilet flange that's attached to the floor. Make sure both bolts are the same distance from the wall behind the toilet. Center the new wax ring on the flange and press it down to make even contact. With the bolts and wax in place, lift the bowl over the flange and guide the closet bolts through the holes in the bowl base. If there is a slight angle in the position of the bowl, straighten it before you press down to fully seat the bowl. Then slide the closet-bolt cap retainer rings and washers over the bolts and thread the nuts on. Tighten the nuts until you feel steady resistance, then push down on the bowl again and tighten the nuts another turn. Do not overtighten these nuts.

Setting the tank

The same package that contained the bowl caps will contain a large rubber spud washer and tank bolts and washers. Press the spud washer over the flush valve spud nut that protrudes from the tank. Then slide a rubber washer onto each tank bolt and push the bolts into the tank holes. If your toilet came with a tank cushion, place it on the bowl now. Set the tank on the bowl so the bolts go through the matching holes in the bowl. Install a washer and nut on each bolt and tighten them slowly, working from one bolt to the other to equalize pressure. Tighten them only until you feel firm resistance.

Clearances for toilet flange

BACK WALL   SIDE WALL

12"   15"

CLOSET FLANGE

Level bowl with shims

SHIM

Making the water connection
Given the choices now available in toilet supply risers, you are likely to choose one of the flexible types and avoid cutting and shaping chrome-plate copper pipe. Flexible supplies cost a little more, but are much easier to use. Just buy one that's the right length for the job.

Riser made of plastic tubing encased in steel mesh

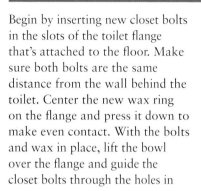

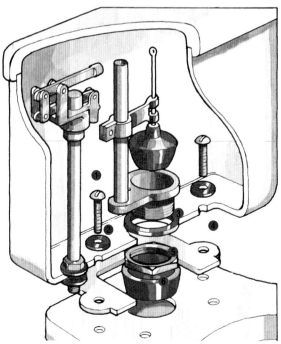

Tank assembly components
1 Tank bolt
2 Rubber washer
3 Tank washer
4 Tank cushion
5 Spud nut
6 Spud washer

The item most likely to wear out and often the most difficult to remove is your toilet seat. The nuts on metal seat bolts almost always rust or corrode to the bolts. When you attempt to loosen these nuts, the bolts, which are molded into the seat hinge, break loose inside the hinge and turn in place. The only alternative left is to saw the bolts off at bowl level with a small hacksaw.

To avoid chipping or scarring the porcelain surface, tape some cardboard on to the toilet rim in front of the seat hinge. By doing this you'll be able to lay the saw blade flat on the bowl and cut under the seat hinge. It's tedious work, but once done it should not need to be done again. Most seats manufactured today use plastic bolts and nuts.

Once you are rid of your old-fashioned seat with its brass bolts, your next replacement will be much easier. When shopping for a seat and lid, choose a painted wooden one. The plastic models on the market are not as sturdy.

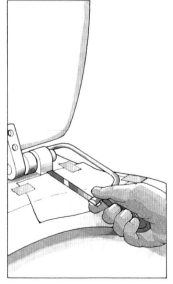

Protect bowl from saw with cardboard scrap

When a toilet is allowed to leak for months at a time, the water almost always damages the floor around it. If you have dry rot around your toilet, you will have to take up the toilet and replace a section of the floor. This is an involved task, but not a difficult one.

Take up the toilet and cut out the rotted flooring with a circular saw. Then measure the area and cut a plywood replacement to fit the removed section. Measure and cut the opening for the toilet flange, keeping in mind that the flange rim must rest on top of the plywood.

Cut the plywood in two pieces so the center of the flange opening is the center of the cut. Slide each plywood half under the flange and nail down. Then screw the flange to the new floor.

Slide plywood under flange

Toilet flanges do occasionally break. The repair method depends mostly upon the material of the flange and soil pipe connected to it. Cast-iron flanges break most easily because of the nature of the metal. Brass flanges can also become brittle with age and break; copper flanges will tear out at the slots. Plastic flanges can also tear or break at the slots. And any flange connected to a lead riser is easily threatened. If a toilet is tightened down too much, either the stool or the flange will likely break.

Replacing a cast-iron flange

If your cast-iron flange breaks at one of its side slots, you may be able to effect a quick fix that is also permanent: You can buy a simple strap-metal repair item that works quite well in most situations. The strap is curved and shaped to slide under an existing flange. Just insert a closet bolt through the repair strap and slide the strap under the broken side of the flange. The strap is usually long enough to catch under the remaining edges of the existing flange. The pressure from the closet bolt keeps the repair piece tightly in place.

If your cast-iron flange is badly broken, you will need to replace it. To do so, first take up the toilet and clean the excess wax from the flange. If the flange is screwed to the floor, remove the screws. Then use an old screwdriver and hammer to pry the lead out of the joint between the flange and soil pipe.

Hammer the screwdriver into the lead about ½ inch deep and pry up as you go.

Once you have the old flange out, slide the new flange over the soil pipe and make sure that both closet-bolt slots are the same distance from the back wall. Then use heavy-duty nonferrous wood screws to fasten the flange to the floor. To make a leakproof lead-and-oakum joint, push oakum into the joint and press it down so that it seats against the rim of the flange. Then use a hammer and packing iron to pack the oakum completely around the joint. Add more oakum until you have filled the joint two-thirds full. Finally, pack the remainder of the joint with lead wool until the hub is full.

Repair strap and broken flange

Removing a cast-iron flange and lead riser

Many older homes have cast-iron flanges connected to lead risers. Because lead is soft and becomes brittle with age, this combination should be replaced. Lead risers were used because lead is easier to work than cast iron. One end of the riser is bonded to a cast-iron insert that fits inside the nearest hub of cast-iron waste pipe. The other end comes through the bathroom floor and is flared out under a flat, cast-iron flange. The best solution is to take out the flange and most of the lead riser and convert to plastic.

First remove the flange from the floor. Then cut the lead where it meets the cast-iron insert. Install a 4-by-3-inch no-hub coupling over the insert and continue with a suitable length of plastic pipe topped off with a plastic flange. Remember to keep the closet bolt holes 12 inches from the wall.

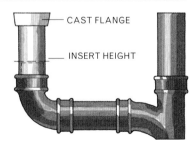
CAST FLANGE
INSERT HEIGHT
Flange connection with a lead riser

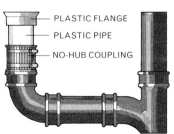
PLASTIC FLANGE
PLASTIC PIPE
NO-HUB COUPLING
Flange connection with a plastic pipe

Plastic flanges

On plastic flanges, usually one of the slots breaks or tears loose. If the ceiling below your stool is open, such as in a basement, the easiest way to remove a plastic stool flange is to cut the waste pipe just below the flange. Then remove the flange screws and pull the damaged flange out.

Buy a new flange and a coupling. Glue the new flange to a short stub of pipe and join the pipe to the waste line with a coupling. Make sure the bolt slots are the same distance from the back wall before the glue sets. Then screw the flange to the floor and reset the toilet.

If the waste pipe is 4-inch plastic, use a reciprocating saw to cut the lip of the flange from above. Saw around the joint where the top of the soil pipe meets the flange, then glue the new flange inside the waste pipe and screw the flange to the floor.

Toilet repairs

Toilet types

Toilets are a marvel of mechanical simplicity. With only a few moving parts, your toilet is responsible for nearly half the water used in your home every day. It is easy to take toilets for granted, until they start to malfunction. Then we wonder how so few parts can cause so much trouble.

When you come to understand how a toilet really works, repair will no longer be a mystery. Mechanically, the components of a two-piece toilet haven't changed much since the turn of the century. The changes that have been made are generally modest, mostly stemming from the need to conserve water. You can expect toilets in the future to flush with much less water than they use today. Even so, the age-old concept of gravity-flow flush valves and float-controlled ballcocks is likely to endure.

How toilets work

The typical toilet has only three mechanical components: trip lever, flush valve, and ballcock. The design of the toilet allows it to work so simply.

A two-piece toilet consists of a bowl, which rests on the floor, and a tank, which mounts on the bowl. The bowl contains a built-in trap that holds a consistent amount of water. The water trapped in the bowl keeps the bowl clean and keeps sewer gases from escaping from waste pipes.

The rim of the bowl is hollow. Water from the tank rushes into the rim and sprays through holes on its underside (and through a tube exiting opposite the drain opening). These holes are drilled at an angle, which causes the water to stream down the sides of the bowl at an angle. This angled spray serves two very important purposes.

It cleans the sides of the bowl, and it starts the water in the bowl spiraling into the trap, which starts the siphoning action that pulls the water out of the bowl, over the trap, and into the waste pipe. Once the water in the bowl begins siphoning over the trap, the water draining out of the tank keeps the siphon going until all the waste is gone. When the tank is empty and the flow is stopped, the siphon breaks, which causes the water climbing the trap to fall back into the bowl.

The tank is less a matter of design than of mechanics. All the tank does is hold water. Water is brought into the tank through a ballcock and is released through a flush valve. When you press down on the flush lever, a chain pulls a ball or flapper off the flush valve opening. Water then rushes into the bowl. The water level drops in the tank, which lowers the ballcock float, which opens the ballcock to incoming water. When most of the water passes through the flush valve, the ball or flapper settles back into place and the tank begins to fill again. When the water level reaches a certain point, the float shuts off the incoming flow of water through the ballcock.

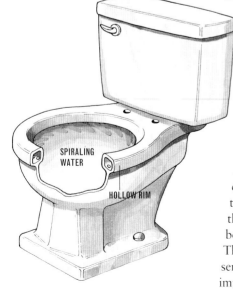

SPIRALING WATER

HOLLOW RIM

This early toilet design features a separate elevated tank mounted high on the wall. The flush lever was activated by pulling on a chain.

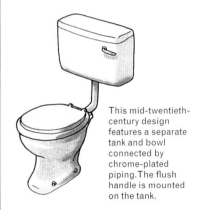

This mid-twentieth-century design features a separate tank and bowl connected by chrome-plated piping. The flush handle is mounted on the tank.

This contemporary toilet has a much more compact design. It still has a separate tank, but it rests directly on the bowl and it uses less water than its predecessors. No connective piping is needed. The flush lever is still mounted on the front of the tank.

Repairing a ballcock

Choosing a replacement ballcock

When a ballcock assembly wears out, some external component may break or the diaphragm may become too porous or brittle to make the seal. If an external part breaks, you will have to replace the entire ballcock assembly. If the internal seals wear out, you can replace them without replacing the ballcock. The type of ballcock you have, its age, and the convenient availability of parts will have a lot to do with the repair choices you make.

Replacing a ballcock seal

If the ballcock in your toilet is made of brass and has been in service for many years, you should probably replace it. If your toilet is not that old, or if the ballcock is made of plastic, you can probably get by with changing only the diaphragm seals. Start by shutting off the water below the toilet, or at the meter, and flushing the water. Remove the screws on the diaphragm cover and lift off the float-arm assembly and cover. Place them aside. Remove all rubber washers and gaskets from the float-arm assembly and diaphragm and examine the rim of the diaphragm seat. If you can feel pits in the rim

surface, you will have to replace the entire ballcock. If not, take the rubber washers and gaskets to your local plumbing outlet and buy replacement parts to match them.

Clean the entire mechanism to remove any sediment or rust flakes that may have entered through the supply piping. Then cover the new rubber washers and gaskets with heatproof grease, press them in place, and reattach the cover.

Remove diaphragm cover for access

Still widely used is the traditional brass ballcock with float-arm assembly. The term "ballcock" refers to this specific mechanism. The ball on the end of a float arm rises and falls with the water level, thus closing and opening a valve-cock mechanism. This design was used for so long that all mechanisms that fill a tank are often called ballcocks, even though their floats are not ball-shaped or their valves float-operated.

The Fluidmaster design offers two advantages. It comes with antisiphon valves, and it can be easily twisted apart at valve level if you need to clean the diaphragm. (In older homes, mineral deposits from aging pipes often lodge under the diaphragm.) A third design, called a Fillmaster, uses no float at all. Instead, a built-in regulator allows a measured amount of water into the tank and then shuts off automatically. This lets you easily adjust the water volume to meet the needs of the type of toilet you have.

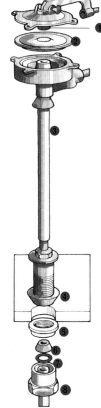

Brass ballcock components

1 Valve
2 Diaphragm
3 Refill tube
4 Rubber gasket
5 Jamb nut
6 Cone washer
7 Washer
8 Supply riser

Replacing a ballcock

To install a replacement ballcock, first shut off the water. Then flush the bowl and sponge all remaining water out of the tank. Remove the nut that attaches the ballcock to the supply line and the jamb nut that holds the ballcock to the tank. Pull the ballcock straight up and out of the tank. If putty was used, scrape the residue from the bottom of the tank and clean the area with a rag.

To insure a leakproof connection, apply pipe-joint compound to the new ballcock gasket. Then insert the shank of the ballcock through the hole in the tank. From underneath the tank, thread the jamb nut onto the ballcock and tighten it with your fingers. Before tightening the nut

completely, make sure that the float will not rub against the tank wall or catch on the flush valve overflow. Then tighten the jamb nut with a wrench until the gasket is flattened out and the nut feels tight. Fasten the refill tube to the inside of the overflow tube.

It's a good idea to replace the supply riser when you install a new ballcock. Be sure to coat the cone washer on the top of the riser with pipe-joint compound before you attach it to the ballcock.

Adjusting the performance of the new ballcock is done by bending the brass float arm. Bend it up for higher water, down for lower water. The water level should be about one inch below the overflow tube.

Remove supply line and jamb nut to free ballcock

Lift old ballcock out and linstall new one

Fluidmaster valve

Flush valves

Flush valves can be very persistent sources of trouble. Luckily, most flush-valve problems can be corrected with replacement tank balls.

Adjusting a tank ball

For a flush valve to work properly, the tank ball must drop smoothly and seat tightly. This motion is controlled by the lift wires, which can be adjusted in two ways. The trip lever has multiple holes for attaching the upper lift wire. Pick the one that yields the best results. The travel of the bottom wire is controlled by the lift wire guide that is clamped to the overflow pipe. Loosen this clamp to move the guide.

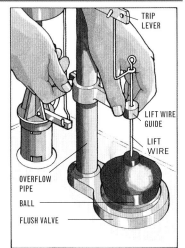

Flush-valve components
1 Plastic cup
2 Bowl refill tube
3 Trip lever
4 Overflow tube
5 Lift wires
6 Lift-wire guide
7 Tank ball
8 Flush valve
9 Lever
10 Valve seat
11 Lift rod
12 Clip

Replacing a tank ball and assembly

If your tank ball is damaged and needs to be replaced, start by shutting off the water to the toilet. Then reach into the tank, hold the ball still, and unthread the lift wire from the top of the ball. If the ball is very old and brittle, the threaded inset may tear out of the rubber. If this happens, hold the inset with pliers and back the lift wire out.

With the tank ball removed, check the valve seat for calcium buildup and sand the valve seat if necessary. Then slide the lower lift wire through the lift wire guide and thread it into the new tank ball. If either lift wire is bent, replace it.

The lift-wire guide is mounted on the overflow tube and controls

the travel of the lower lift wire. You adjust it by loosening its clamp screw and moving the guide's position. Sometimes this screw can be very stubborn. Work carefully with it to avoid breaking off the overflow tube in the flush valve. If this happens, you can replace the tube if you put in the effort. But in most cases it makes more sense to replace the whole flush valve.

Hold the upper lift wire next to the trip level and move the wire and ball up and down to determine where the upper wire should be fastened. Feed the upper wire through the best hole and bend it over on the other side. Then fill the tank with water and flush the toilet several times. Adjust as needed.

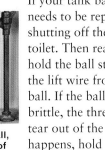

To remove ball, first lift it out of flush valve

Hold ball firmly and unthread the lift wire

Some flush valves use a flapper mechanism instead of a tank ball. Both types serve the same purpose: holding water in the tank. If a flapper no longer holds water, usually you need to install a new one.

To replace a flapper, first shut off the water to the tank. Then reach into the tank and carefully pull the rubber eyelets off the flush-valve pegs. Disconnect the chain from the trip lever and discard the old flapper. It's a good idea to scour the seat rim with steel wool or emery cloth to remove any calcium buildup.

Some flush valves have no pegs to mount the flapper. In this case, slide the collar of the flapper over the overflow tube until it seats against the bottom of the flush valve. If your flush valve does have pegs, hook the flapper's eyelets over these pegs. Universal flappers, which work for both types of valves, are commonly available. They include instructions for both installations. After the flapper is in place, hook the chain to the trip lever so that there is not more than ½-inch slack in the chain.

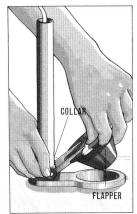

To install flapper, slide collar to bottom of tube

Attach flapper chain to hole in trip lever

Faulty flush valves

Replacing a faulty trip lever

If a flush-valve seat is pitted or defective in any way, replacing the flapper or tank ball will do little good. The best solution is to separate the tank from the bowl and replace the entire flush valve. If this seems too intimidating, you can install a replacement seat over the defective seat.

Dealing with a faulty flush valve

Installing a replacement seat
A seat replacement kit consists of a stainless-steel seat rim, a flapper-ball carriage, a flapper ball, and epoxy putty. To install a seat replacement kit, you must first remove the flapper or tank ball and dry the defective flush valve completely. Press the new seat over the old so the epoxy is flattened evenly against both surfaces. 0Then allow the epoxy to dry.

Press new replacement seat into flush valve

Replacing a flush valve
A more permanent and much preferred solution is to replace the entire flush valve. To do this, you must first remove the tank from the bowl. Because tank bolts are likely to break in the process, you should buy new tank bolts when you buy the replacement flush valve. And it's a good idea to replace the spud washer as long as the tank is being removed.

Flush the bowl and then sponge out all the water in the tank. Disconnect the water-supply tube at the ballcock. Remove the tank bolts that hold the tank to the bowl. Lift the tank straight up and lay it on its side on the floor. Remove the large rubber spud washer from the flush-valve spud. Use a spud wrench or large adjustable pliers to undo the spud nut from the old flush-valve assembly.

If any putty or pipe-joint compound is stuck to the tank bottom, scrape it off with a putty knife and sand the area around the opening. Then apply pipe-joint compound to the new spud washer.

Insert the flush valve through the tank opening and fasten it in place with the new spud nut. Make sure that the overflow tube is not in the way of the float arm inside the tank. Then press the new rubber spud washer over the spud nut and set the tank back on the bowl.

Apply pipe-joint compound to the rubber washers on the tank bolts and slide the bolts through the tank holes and bowl holes. (Some tanks require that you fasten the tank bolts to the tank with a second set of nuts and washers before setting the tank in place. Other models require rubber spacers, or a cushion, between the tank and the bowl.) Then tighten the tank bolts a little at a time until the tank rests firmly on the bowl, and reconnect the water-supply line.

Finally, attach the flapper or tank ball to the overflow tube and make any necessary adjustments so the flapper or ball seats properly on the flush valve. After the toilet has been flushed several times satisfactorily, check for tank leaks by running your hand under the tank and around the tank bolts. If you find a few drips, tighten the tank bolts.

Replacing a trip lever is not difficult, but the left-hand threads of the retaining nut have stumped many beginner plumbers. The threads are machined on the shank counterclockwise so that the downward motion of the flush lever will not loosen the nut.

Take the lid off the tank and use an adjustable wrench to loosen the retaining nut. When the nut is loose, slide it off of the trip lever. (Some models have set screws instead of retaining nuts.) Then pull the lever out through the tank opening.

To install a new trip lever, feed the lever into the opening until the handle seats. Then slide the nut over the lever until it makes a right-angle turn and rests against the threads of the shank. Tighten the nut and connect the flapper chain or tank-ball wire to the most convenient hole in the lever. Test and make any needed adjustments.

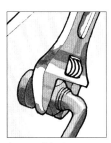

Loosen trip-lever nut by turning clockwise

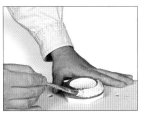

Slide the new trip lever through the tank hole

Tighten the nut on the handle threads

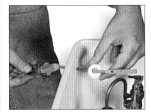

Coat the spud washer with pipe-joint compound

Attach the tank to the bowl with tank bolts

Maintaining toilets

Cleaning toilet-rim holes

Dealing with sweating tanks

Condensation appears on the outside of a toilet tank when cold water from the water system meets the warm humid air of a bathroom. The water that collects on the surface of the tank eventually falls to the floor, often causing water damage over time.

Air-conditioned homes do not tend to have tank-sweating problems because air conditioners dehumidify as they cool. If your home is not air-conditioned, your best alternative is to insulate the tank from the inside. There are polystyrene insulating liners on the market, but you can just as easily make your own, using

½-inch polystyrene or foam rubber. Drain and dry the tank. Cut a piece for each wall and several pieces for the bottom of the tank. Then glue them in place with silicone cement and be sure to allow the glue to dry for a full day.

You can also reduce the temperature extremes by mixing hot water with the cold before it enters the tank. This method wastes hot water, of course, and unless you install a check valve on the hot-water side of the connection, the other fixtures in your home can back-siphon some of the heated water through their cold-water lines.

A temperature valve is available for this purpose. In a typical installation, the temperature valve should be installed just below the ballcock. You attach the cold-water supply to this valve. Then you tap into the hot-water supply of your lavatory and run a ⅜-inch soft copper line to the temperature valve. If you have access from below, in an unfinished basement for example, you can tap into the hot-water line below the floor.

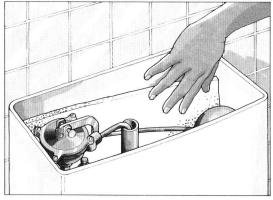

Glue foam rubber or polystyrene to the inside of the tank

Repairing wall-mounted toilet tanks

Repairing a leaking flush ell
Loosen the nuts and wrap the threads with sealant tape.

Many older toilets have wall-mounted tanks that are joined to their bowls by means of a 90-degree pipe, called a "flush ell." While the working parts of these toilets are the same as in newer models, dealing with flush ells requires special care. When a flush ell leaks, carefully undo the nuts with a pipe wrench and clean the threads and the ell thoroughly. Then wrap the threads with Teflon sealant tape and tighten the nuts in place again. When tightening the

spud nut, be sure to hold on to the ell firmly to avoid cracking it.

Because wall-mounted tank toilets waste so much water, and because their flush ells make them harder to repair, you should think about replacing them when they need extensive work. For minor repairs, choose methods that do not require taking off the tank. For example, instead of replacing a worn flush valve, install a stainless-steel flush valve seat replacement.

Every toilet bowl has a rim, and most rims are filled with holes that allow the water from the tank to wash the sides of the bowl before going down the drain. If your toilet's flush seems sluggish and the bowl doesn't clean well, the rim holes are probably restricted or clogged. Often, this is the result of calcified mineral deposits left by hard water. To remove these calcified minerals, pour vinegar into the overflow tube inside the tank. Let it stand for about 30 minutes.

After the vinegar has had a chance to loosen the deposits, ream each hole with a wire. A 1-foot length of coiled 12-gauge electrical wire works well for this job. But if some holes are heavily clogged, use an Allen wrench as a reaming tool. Use a hand mirror to see under the rim. Because porcelain can chip easily, take your time and don't exert too much force.

It's also a good idea to use a wire to clean out the siphon jet hole at the bottom of the bowl. This hole can be clogged from mineral deposits too.

Clean toilet rim holes with an Allen wrench

Use a wire to clean siphon jet hole

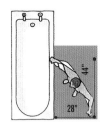

F or many years, bathtub designs consisted of various size freestanding tubs. Today, most tubs are of standard dimensions and are built into the bathroom walls with an apron covering the side of the tub left exposed. Except for whirlpools, basic designs have changed very little in the last forty years, but some important material changes have taken place. Tubs today can be made of enameled cast iron, porcelain-covered steel, or molded fiberglass. The installation of tubs, however, remains much the same as it has always been.

Installing a built-in tub

To install a tub, you will need a framed opening that is 60 1/16 inches long by at least 31 inches deep. On the drain-opening side, cut a hole in the floor that is 8 inches wide by 12 inches long. Center this hole 15 inches from the back wall. Then nail blocking between the studs all around the tub, centering the blocking 14 inches above the floor.

Slide the tub into the opening slowly. Keep your feet and fingers out of the way. If your tub is made of fiberglass or steel, it should move pretty easily. But if your tub is a 375-pound cast-iron model, you may have to pry it into place with a 2x4.

To attach a steel or fiberglass tub, just screw through the lip of the tub and into the blocking you installed between the studs. Cast-iron tubs have no lip and are held in place by the subflooring and wall finish alone.

Minor tub-surface damage can be repaired with touchup kits. But major resurfacing should be done by professionals.

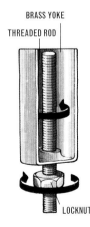

Installing a waste and overflow drain

The waste and overflow drain you buy will come in several pieces. Start by locating the drain shoe, drain gasket, and drain strainer. Wrap a small roll of plumber's putty around the flange of the strainer. Then reach below the tub and hold the drain shoe against the tub opening with its rubber gasket sandwiched between the drain shoe and the tub. Thread the strainer into the drain shoe.

Next, assemble the overflow tube, tripwaste tee, and tailpiece, and connect the tee to the drain shoe with the compression nuts provided. You can also attach the tailpiece to the drain trap at this time.

When the waste and overflow components are assembled, you will be ready to install and adjust the tripwaste mechanism. Feed the plunger into the overflow tube and fasten the coverplate screws.

Adjusting a tripwaste

There are two basic tripwaste designs. One has a plunger cylinder attached to the end of the lift linkage. In the down position, this cylinder slides into the tee and closes it. The other features a pop-up lever and plug in the drain opening of the strainer. When the spring is in the down position, the pop-up lever pushes the plug up and drains the tub.

Pop-up tripwaste
Pull stopper from drain to adjust.

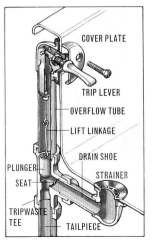

COVER PLATE
TRIP LEVER
OVERFLOW TUBE
LIFT LINKAGE
DRAIN SHOE
PLUNGER
SEAT
STRAINER
TRIPWASTE TEE
TAILPIECE

Typical plunger-type tripwaste and overflow

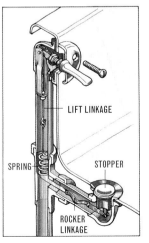

LIFT LINKAGE
SPRING
STOPPER
ROCKER LINKAGE

Typical pop-up tripwaste and overflow

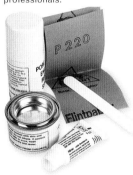

BRASS YOKE
THREADED ROD
LOCKNUT

Plunger tripwaste
Pull plunger from overflow hole to adjust. Turn locknut as needed.

Maintaining bathtubs

Maintaining tub tile walls

Eventually, every tiled tub/shower wall will need repair, but you can extend the life of your tile with a few simple maintenance procedures. The danger signs are loose or missing grout and excessive mildew in grout joints. To regrout a tiled wall, start by digging all soft or loose grout from between tiles with a grout-removal tool. These are available from any tile outlet. All joints that need regrouting should be scraped to a depth of at least 1/16 inch. Then wipe away the loose grout.

With the tile prepared, select a small container of premixed, ready-to-use grout and force a liberal amount into each prepared joint with your finger. Use a damp sponge to smooth the grout. Wipe in large diagonal patterns until the grout is uniform. Then allow it to set for one-half hour and wipe the surface again to remove any residue. After the grout has cured for 24 hours, apply clear silicone sealer to the entire wall with a soft cloth.

Replacing ceramic tiles

When water is allowed to seep behind tiles, it can ruin both the tile mastic and the drywall. Eventually, tiles will loosen and fall out. To replace them, you may need to remove all tiles that have come in contact with moisture and replace a section of drywall.

Use a knife or screwdriver to pry under the tiles. If tiles come up easily, take them out. Then cut out the affected drywall and nail a new piece of moisture-resistant drywall in its place. If the edges fit together neatly, you will not have to tape the seams. Prime the new drywall with clear sealer or oil-base paint and allow the primer to dry completely.

To strip the paper and mastic from the removed tile, soak each tile in very hot water and scrape it clean with a putty knife. Lay the tiles out on the floor in the order in which they will go back on. Apply wall-grade tile mastic to the wall or tile with a notched trowel. A 1/8-inch notch will provide enough gap in the cement to hold the tile to the wall.

With the cement in place, press the old tiles back onto the wall. Clean away any tile cement from the tile surfaces and allow the cement to cure for 72 hours. (If you grout the joints too soon, the gases escaping from the cement will cause pinholes to appear in the grout.) When the cement has cured, grout the new tile joints and seal the entire wall with clear silicone sealer.

Most tub/shower valves on the market come with a diverter spout and showerhead. Start by installing the faucet body. Bring 1/2-inch copper water-supply pipe up in the tub wall to a height of 28 inches. Then cut a 44-inch length of copper for the shower riser and a 4 1/2-inch length for the tub spout nipple. Thread or solder the valve in place, close enough to the wall so that the coverplate screws will reach through the tile and drywall and into the faucet. Then solder a sweat/FIP fitting, called a "drop-eared ell," to the shower riser and to the spout leg. Temporarily install the showerhead and tub spout and turn on both the hot and cold sides of the valve to check for leaks.

After checking for leaks, remove the showerhead and tub spout and finish the walls with drywall and tile. Thread the showerhead into its fitting with Teflon sealant tape. To install the spout, measure from the surface of the tile to 3/8 inch inside the spout fitting and buy a 1/2-inch nipple that length. Wrap sealant tape around both ends of the nipple and thread the nipple into the spout fitting. Then turn the spout onto the nipple and caulk around the spout and faucet coverplate.

Cleaning a tub drain

Often slow-draining tripwastes are partially clogged or need only minor adjustments. Start by undoing the screws that hold the coverplate to the overflow opening and taking the coverplate off. Then, pull the tripwaste linkage up and out of the overflow tube. Clean any hair buildup from the mechanism. On the tripwaste lift linkage you will see either adjustment slots or a threaded adjustment rod with a locknut. If you have a slot adjustment, pinch the two bottom wires together and move them up or down into the next slot level. If your tripwaste has a threaded

adjustment, loosen the locknut and turn it up or down about 1/8 inch and retighten the locknut. Then slide the tripwaste back into the overflow and replace the coverplate.

If you do not find a clog at the tripwaste mechanism, you will have to snake the overflow pipe. Because tubs are snaked through the overflow and not through the drain, you will need to remove the coverplate and tripwaste components. Feed a hand snake into the overflow until you feel resistance at the trap bend. When you feel the trap, start cranking the snake in a clockwise direction while pushing

the cable slightly. After you crank through the trap, pull the snake out and replace the tripwaste and coverplate.

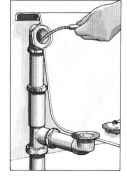

Snake drain through the overflow pipe

Installing showers

Shower stalls come in several varieties and, these days, in quite a few different colors. All-metal or plastic free-standing showers are considered the low end of the market. They can be installed anywhere near a floor drain and are popular in unfinished basements. They are often thought of as utility showers. One-piece fiberglass stalls come in different sizes and colors and are built into framed walls. They are popular in finished bathrooms, both upstairs and down. They always drain into dedicated traps and are plumbed conventionally. A more traditional shower consists of a separate pan built into a framed wall and plumbed into a dedicated trap. The framed walls are covered with moisture-resistant drywall or concrete board and finished with ceramic tile, molded plastic, or fiberglass shower walls.

A free-standing shower stall

Installing a free-standing shower

A free-standing shower consists of a raised pan, three wall panels, corner braces, a drain spud, a valve, and a showerhead. All of these parts will come in a box and must be assembled on site.

Start by setting up the pan and plumbing the drainpipe to the nearest floor drain. Then install the walls and corner braces and fasten the walls to the pan

according to directions supplied with the shower.

Next, assemble the valve and shower riser and mount the valve and showerhead to the plumbing wall of the shower. Some free-standing shower stalls will have predrilled valve holes, but other models will have to be drilled. The manufacturer usually supplies a template for this job.

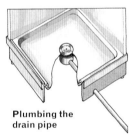

Run surface piping to the nearest floor drain.

Plumbing the drain pipe

Installing a one-piece fiberglass shower

To install a one-piece fiberglass shower, start by framing the walls. The width of the opening should not be more than 1/16 inch wider than the width of the fiberglass stall. The depth of the opening should exceed the front drywall lip of the shower by more than 2 inches. With the framing completed, cut the drainhole in the floor. To do this, take the measurements from the bottom of the shower stall to find the center of the drain, and make the opening at least 5 inches in diameter so you will have room to work.

Next, install the drain assembly in the pan opening. Wrap the underside of the drain flange with plumber's putty and press it into

the opening. Then slide the gasket in place from below and tighten the spud nut.

With the drain installed, you are ready to set the shower in its frame. Because fiberglass shower floors tend to flex, it is a good idea to support the floor with a little perlite plaster. Mix enough of this plaster to cover the wooden floor 1 inch deep and about 1½ feet extending around the drainhole. Then set the shower in place on top of the plaster. Level the shower walls and step into the shower to settle the base into the plaster. Nail the lip of the shower walls to the studs with galvanized roofing nails and connect the drain trap below the floor.

With the stall in place, measure for the shower-valve cut. The valve should be 48 inches off the floor and the showerhead should be 6 feet or more above the floor. Use a holesaw to cut the shower-valve holes. Solder the shower valve, supply lines, and showerhead riser together and mount this assembly on the framed wall. Make sure the valve extends through the shower wall. With the valve in place, install the showerhead. Then connect the water-supply lines to the water system and test the solder joints under full pressure to make sure there are no leaks. Install and finish drywall on the exposed framed walls and paint.

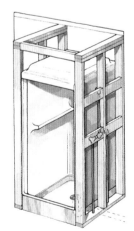

Framing the opening
Frame an opening to match the size of the shower.

Hardboard shield
Use a piece of hardboard to protect the shower when driving nails through the lip.

Installing showerheads

Installing a shower pan

Like a one-piece shower, a shower pan is installed in a framed opening. Simply frame the stall as you would with a one-piece shower and cut the drain opening in the floor. Install the drain flange in the pan, using putty under the flange, and set the pan in place.

Many shower pans are designed so the drainpipe from the trap extends up, through the drain flange, to just below the drain screen. To seal this joint, insert a rubber gasket around the pipe. Push it in with your hands or tap it with a hammer and packing tool.

With the pan installed and connected to the drain line, install the valve and showerhead piping in the framed wall. Test the piping and cover the walls with moisture-resistant drywall. Then cover the drywall with ceramic tile or a molded shower surround.

Trace the drain opening of shower pan on floor

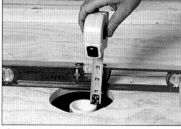

Check height of drain riser to top of shower pan

Install rubber gasket to seal drain riser to pan

Installing a tub or shower surround

Shower pan
This versatile fixture is a good way to start a stall-shower installation. Once you have the pan installed properly, you can add drywall and ceramic tile above to cover the walls. Or you can install one of the many different shower surround wall kits.

Molded fiberglass or plastic tub and shower surrounds are easy to install and offer long-term durability. The appeal of these molded shower walls is that they have very few seams that can leak. The only situation that inhibits the use of surrounds is crooked walls. Even with out-of-plumb walls, a little bottom edge trimming will create an effective seal.

Most tub or shower surrounds come in three pieces. You will have to cut the valve and spout access holes, but beyond that, they are ready to go. Before installing any of the panels, put a level on all walls and on the top of the tub or shower pan to make sure they are plumb and level. If all is straight and level, mark the exact center of the back wall in the room. Then mark the center of the back shower wall panel.

Apply several beads of panel adhesive to the back of the center panel. Then peel the paper from the adhesive strips around the edges, if present. Lift the panel up to the

back tub or shower pan rim so that the bottom of the panel is an inch away from the wall. Rest the panel on several matchsticks laid on the back rim. When the center of the panel is aligned with the center of the back wall, press the bottom of the panel against the wall. Work from bottom to top until the adhesive strip has sealed the entire panel. Then rub the panel firmly with the palm of your hand to flatten the panel to the wall.

Next, install the corner panel opposite the plumbing wall. Use the same method you used for the back panel, but press the corner in first. The corner panel will lap the back panel by several inches.

To cut the valve handles and tub spout in the plumbing wall panel, remove the spout and handles and measure from the tub rim and inside corner. Use a holesaw

to cut the openings. Even a small cutting error will ruin the panel, so double-check all measurements before cutting. With the holes made, slide the panel over the valve stems and spout pipe to make sure everything fits. Then apply panel adhesive, peel the paper from the adhesive strips and press the panel in place, starting at the corner.

When the adhesive dries, caulk the bottom seam and the valve flanges with white silicone sealant and both corners with latex tub and tile caulk.

Apply adhesive to panel back and install panel

Cut shower-pipe hole in panel with holesaw

Water heaters

Water heaters are fairly simple appliances, but when problems arise, they can present an array of confusing symptoms. Because problems can occur in any part of your hot-water systems, don't limit your investigation to the heater alone. The diagnostic charts on the next page will help you locate the source of your hot-water troubles.

The piping system

In some cases, water-heater problems turn out to be piping problems instead. For example, high operating costs can often be traced to dripping faucets or leaking pipes. Several dripping faucets in your home can waste hundreds of gallons of water a year. A simple, inexpensive faucet repair can pay for itself quickly, in the energy it saves.

Long uninsulated piping runs also waste hot water. When you draw water from a faucet at the end of a run, hot water from the tank must first push the cooled water through the pipe. This not only wastes water but energy as well. Uninsulated pipes dissipate heat much as a radiator does. To keep the energy you buy from escaping through the walls of hot-water pipes, you should consider insulating all hot-water lines.

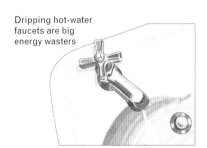

Dripping hot-water faucets are big energy wasters

Problems inside the tank

An aging water system can carry sediment into a tank, or sediment may collect in flakes of calcium and lime. In electric models, sediment-covered heating elements will burn out quickly. In gas water heaters, sediment accumulates in the bottom of the tank and forms a barrier between the heat source and the water. Not only does sediment make your heater very inefficient but air bubbles created by the heat percolate through the sediment and cause a continuous rumbling sound. So if your electric heater burns up lower elements frequently, or if your heater rumbles, sediment may be the culprit.

To remove sediment, drain as much water as possible from the tank. Then turn the water supply on and allow the new water to flush through the drain valve for a few minutes.

Dip tubes

A dip tube is a plastic pipe that delivers incoming cold water to the heat source near the tank bottom.

Occasionally, a dip tube will slip through the cold-water inlet fitting and fall into the tank. When this happens, cold water entering the tank is drawn through the hot-water outlet without being heated. To replace a dip tube, disconnect the inlet pipe from the tank. Then slide a new dip tube into the fitting and reconnect the inlet pipe.

Anode rods

New water heaters are equipped with magnesium anode rods that prevent rust from developing in the porcelain tank lining. An anode rod acts as a sacrificial element to draw rust and corrosion to itself. These rods are usually troublefree, but problems can occur when water has an unusually high concentration of dissolved mineral salts. As a result, the water will have a gassy odor or taste. To correct this, replace the magnesium rod with an aluminum rod.

Relief valves

A relief valve keeps a heater from exploding in the event a

thermostat becomes stuck. When pressure builds and the water gets too hot, the relief valve opens until the pressure is equalized. However, the spring mechanism in some valves weakens with age and the valves release water with any slight variation in pressure. To correct this, simply remove the old valve and thread in a new one.

To remove sediment, drain tank with garden hose

To remove anode, unscrew from tank and pull out

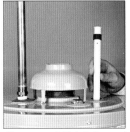

Remove cold inlet pipe and slide dip tube in place

Screw new valve into side of tank

Gas and electric water heaters: symptoms

gas water-heater diagnostic chart

CAUSES	Burner will not light	Burner flame floats—Lifts off	Burner flame yellow—Lazy	Burner flame noisy	Burner flame too high	Burner pops when turned off or on	Flame burns at orifice	Pilot will not stay lit	High operating costs	Insufficient hot water	Slow hot-water recovery	Pounding and steaming at faucet	Dripping relief valve	Thermostat fails to close	Condensation	Combustion odors	Smoking—Carbon formation	Pilot flame too small	Pilot flame too large	SOLUTIONS
Insufficient secondary air		●		●						●						●	●			Provide ventilation
Dirt in main burner orifice	●		●			●	●		●	●	●					●	●	●		Clean—Install dirt trap
Dirt in pilot burner orifice								●										●		Clean—Install dirt trap
Flue clogged		●	●				●	●		●					●	●	●			Remove—Blow clean—Reinstall
Pilot line clogged	●							●										●		Clean—Install dirt trap
Burner line clogged	●		●					●												Clean—Check source and correct
Wrong pilot burner	●							●										●	●	Replace with correct pilot burner
Loose thermocouple								●												Finger-tight plus 1/4 turn
Defective thermocouple lead	●							●												Replace thermocouple
Defective thermostat	●					●					●		●		●					Replace thermostat—(Call plumber)
Improper calibration									●	●	●	●	●	●						Replace—(Call plumber)
Heater in confined area	●	●	●												●	●	●			Install vent in wall or door
Heater not connected to the flue		●	●		●										●	●	●			Provide and connect to proper flue
Sediment or lime in tank									●	●	●		●							Drain and flush—Repeat
Heater too small									●	●	●									Upgrade to larger heater
Gas leaks									●											Check with utility—Repair immediately
Excess draft		●		●					●		●									Check source, stop draft
Long runs of exposed piping									●	●										Insulate hot lines only
Surge from washer solenoid valve													●							Insulate air cushion pipe
Faulty relief valve													●							Install rated T&P valve—Soon
Dip tube broken									●	●	●									Replace dip tube

electric water-heater diagnostic chart

CAUSES	No hot water	Insufficient hot water	Slow hot-water recovery	Steaming and pounding at faucet	High operating costs	Dripping relief valve	Excessive relief valve operation	Condensation	Element failure	Blown fuse, tripped circuit breaker	Service wires charred or hot	Continuous operation	Singing thermostat	Wet heater insulation	Gas odor or taste in water	Fluctuating temperatures	Rusty or discolored water	Rumbling, pounding in tank	SOLUTIONS
No power	●									●									Check fuses, breakers—Reset
Undersize heater		●		●								●				●			Install larger heater
Undersize elements		●	●									●							Replace with rated element
Wrong wiring connections	●	●		●					●	●	●								See manufacturer's instructions
No relief valve				●															Install relief valve—Soon
Leaking faucets		●		●										●					Locate and repair
Leaks around heating elements	●			●			●							●					Tighten tank flange
Sediment or lime in tank		●		●													●	●	Drain and flush—Water treatment?
Lime formation on elements		●	●														●	●	Replace elements
Themostat not flush with tank		●	●	●	●							●	●			●			Reposition
Faulty wiring connection	●	●	●					●	●			●				●			Locate, reconnect
Faulty ground		●	●	●								●							See maker's grounding instructions
Short	●			●				●	●	●									Locate short circuit—Correct
Gas from mangnesium anode rod															●			●	Install aluminum anode rod
Damage from electrolysis																	●		Install dielectric unions
Excessive mineral deposits		●															●		Flush tank—Install water filter
Improper calibration	●	●	●	●	●	●	●						●						Replace thermostat—(Call plumber)
Eroded anode rod															●	●			Replace
Faulty thermostat	●	●	●	●	●	●										●		●	Replace—(Call plumber)
Faulty high limit (ECO)	●	●	●	●								●				●		●	Replace
Open high limit (ECO)	●	●																	Reset button or replace
Dip tube broken		●	●		●											●			Replace dip tube

A typical gas water heater consists of a steel tank, a layer of insulation, and a sheetmetal jacket. The bottom of the tank is heated by a fixed gas burner that is controlled by a thermocouple and a regulator valve. To vent excess heat and noxious fumes, a gas heater tank is equipped with a hollow tube, through its center, that connects to a house flue.

A supply of secondary air

For a gas heater to burn evenly and efficiently it must have an ample supply of combustion air. If your water heater shares space with a furnace and clothes dryer, then a continuous air supply is especially important, because they compete with the heater for air. When a heater is starved for air, the flame will burn orange, jump, and pop. An orange flame means higher operating costs. Be sure that the heater has a sufficient supply of combustion air by opening doors in confined areas or by installing louvered vents in the doors.

A clogged flue

A clogged flue is caused by rust or debris that accumulates at tight bends in the flue piping. A clogged flue is a serious heath hazard. Deadly carbon gases, unable to vent through the flue, are forced into living quarters. An easy way to check that the flue is working properly is to place a burning match, or burning piece of cardboard, near the flue hat while the heater is on. The smoke should be drawn into the flue. To locate an obstruction, turn the heater to pilot and disassemble the vent pipes. Inspect and clean each piece of pipe, then reassemble the flue.

Dirt in gas lines

Dirt in gas lines often makes its way into the heater's control mechanism. A dirty pilot line or burner line will cause the heater to burn unevenly or to stop burning entirely. To clean these lines, disconnect them from the regulator and slide a thin wire through each line. Then blow air through the lines. If dirt is lodged in the gas control valve, call a plumber. Control valves are delicate mechanisms that can be dangerous if serviced improperly.

Gas leaks

If you smell a strong gas odor, it's likely there is a dangerous gas leak. Leave the house immediately and call your gas or utility company. If you smell only a light trace of gas, it may be a leaky pipe joint. To find the leak, brush every joint with a mixture of dish detergent and warm water. Soap bubbles will appear around the leaky joint. Shut off the gas at the meter. Bleed the line at the union located above the heater and ventilate the area.

Take apart the leaking joint and clean the fitting and pipe thoroughly with a wire brush. Then reassemble the parts with pipe-joint compound. Tighten all the joints. Turn on the gas, bleed the air from the line, and retest all the new joints with soap and warm water.

Thermocouple breakdown

A thermocouple is a thick copper wire that has a heat sensor on one end and a plug on the other. Heat from the pilot flame sends a tiny millivolt charge through the wire, which causes the plug to open the control valve. When a thermocouple's sensor burns out, the heater's magnetic safety valve remains closed and the pilot light won't burn. To replace a thermocouple, turn off the gas and disconnect the entire burner assembly from the control valve. Remove the thermocouple from its retainer clip near the pilot and snap a new one in its place. Be sure to position the sensor directly in line with the pilot flame. Finally, reconnect the burner assembly to the control valve.

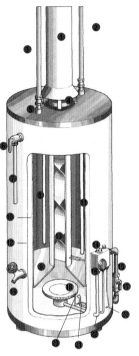

Basic components of a gas water-heater

1 Vent
2 Cold-water inlet
3 Hot-water outlet
4 Flue hat
5 Union
6 Relief valve
7 Discharge pipe
8 Anode rod
9 Water
10 Tank
11 Dip tube
12 Insulation
13 Flue baffle
14 Gas control
15 Gas pipe
16 Temperature control
17 Gas valve
18 Burner
19 Draincock
20 Thermocouple lead
21 Pilot line
22 Burner supply
23 Thermocouple

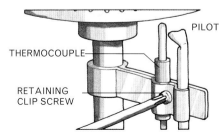

PILOT
THERMOCOUPLE
RETAINING
CLIP SCREW

Loosen clip screw to remove thermocouple

Electric water-heater problems

**Basic components
of an electric
water heater**

1 Cold-water inlet
2 Hot-water outlet
3 Union
4 Power cable
5 Relief valve
6 Discharge pipe
7 Insulation
8 Tank
9 High-limit switch
10 Upper element
11 Upper thermostat
12 Anode rod
13 Dip tube
14 Lower element
15 Lower thermostat
16 Draincock
17 Bracket
18 Element flange
19 Gasket

If your electric water heater fails, first check for burned-out fuses or tripped circuit breakers at the main service panel. If the problem is not in the service panel, go to the heater. Remove the access panels and press the reset button on each thermostat and listen for a ticking noise caused by expansion as the elements begin to heat up. If this procedure doesn't produce hot water, the problem may be in the wiring, thermostats, or elements.

Loose wires

Remove the access panels for both heating elements and check to see if any wire has come loose from its terminal. If a wire is loose or disconnected, turn off the power to the heater, then loosen the terminal screw, bend the end of the wire around it, and tighten the screw.

Defective thermostat element

To determine if the problem is in the element, thermostat, or high-limit protector, test each part with a volt-ohmmeter (VOM). If you do not have a VOM, try simple logic. If the heater produces plenty of warm water but no hot water, then the top element or thermostat is probably defective. If you get a few gallons of very hot water followed by cool water, then the bottom element or thermostat probably needs replacing. Since elements fail much more often than thermostats, assume a faulty element or test with a VOM.

Replacing an element

To replace a defective element, first shut off the power and water supply to the heater. Next, drain the tank to a level below the element to be replaced. Disconnect the wires from the terminals and unscrew the element. Pull the element straight out of the tank. Then clean the gasket surface, coat it lightly with pipe-joint compound and seat a new gasket. Attach the new element to the heater and reconnect the wires to the terminals. (Some elements thread into a threaded tank opening, while others bolt to a gasket flange.) Before turning the power on, fill the tank with water and bleed all trapped air through the faucets. An element that is energized when dry will burn out in seconds.

Finally, replace the insulation, thermostat protection plates, and access panel. Then turn on the power. If after 45 minutes you still don't have sufficient hot water, a replacement thermostat is in order.

Replacing a thermostat

Shut off the power and disconnect the wires from the thermostat's terminals. Pry out the old thermostat and snap the new one into the clip. Then reconnect the wires, replace the insulation, and turn the power back on. Allow both elements to complete their heating cycles and then test the water temperature at the faucets using a meat thermometer. Adjust the thermostat until the water temperature is between 130° and 140° F.

New designs in electric water heaters

For years, electric water heaters have been made with metal storage tanks. All other components were replaceable, but when a tank developed a leak, the entire heater had to be replaced. The longevity of the tank, then, determined the longevity of the heater. While most manufacturers still prefer metal tanks, some offer plastic tanks. Because plastic cannot rust through, and because mineral salts will not adhere to it, this new design has real potential.

Another recent design rejects the principle of storing hot water entirely. The makers of this design maintain that heating and reheating stored water is too wasteful. They offer, instead, a system that heats cold water as it passes through a heating element. In this way, only the water used is heated. With careful use and planning, these units should offer real savings. If you regularly take showers while your clothes washer or dishwasher is operating, then this system may have trouble keeping up. In any case, consider your needs before investing.

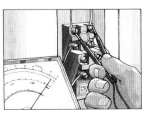

**Troubleshoot thermostat
with an ohmmeter**

**Adjust temperature setting
with screwdriver**

Water softeners

The water we pump into our homes varies greatly in quality from region to region, and even from well to well. The degree of mineral content in groundwater accounts for these differences and can also account for health and plumbing problems, too. Most municipal systems provide water that falls within tolerable limits of hardness and dissolved mineral salts. Others, especially rural systems, do not. When mineral levels are too high, water must be treated or filtered to bring it within acceptable tolerances for home use.

To install softener, join union stubs to risers

Water softeners

The purpose of a water softener is to substitute sodium for calcium, magnesium, or iron. These minerals, in sufficient concentrations, can cause clogged pipes and appliances and can give drinking water a foul smell. Water softeners neutralize these minerals, which makes conditioned water feel softer. It helps eliminate soap scum on fixtures and reduces the amount of mineral sediment in water heaters.

If soap does not dissolve easily in your water or if mineral buildup occurs on your fixtures, then you may need a softener. Have your water tested by a local lab to get a good reading of the mineral content.

If you do need a water softener, consider isolating your main cold-water drinking faucets and your outdoor hydrants. Softeners naturally raise the salt content of drinking water, which presents some health risks, especially for those on low-sodium diets. And, of course it doesn't make sense to pay for soft water that you use to wash the car or water the garden.

The easiest installation in a home with finished basement ceilings is to tie the intake of the softener to the inlet line of your water heater. With a hot-water-only installation, you get soft water where you need it most, in your clothes washer and dishwasher. You will also get some soft water in your tub/shower or wherever you mix hot and cold water.

But, for a more complete installation, you should tie the softener into the incoming water

trunk line before it reaches any branch fittings. To isolate cold-water drinking faucets and outdoor sillcocks or hydrants, cut and cap the branch fittings that serve these lines and tie all hard-water lines in at a new location, somewhere between the meter and the soft-water inlet fitting.

All water softeners must be equipped with a three-way bypass valve. You can buy a three-way valve and splice it into the inlet and outlet lines of the softener. Or you can make one yourself, by first installing a separate globe valve in the inlet and outlet lines. Then install a tee in each pipe above these valves, joined by a third valve that acts as a bypass. When the softener is in service, the two line valves are open and the center valve is closed. When the softener is not in service, the two line valves are closed and the center valve is opened to allow water to pass through without going to the softener.

Attach purge line and overflow tube to unit head

Connect riser-pipe unions to bypass valve

Push softener into place against wall

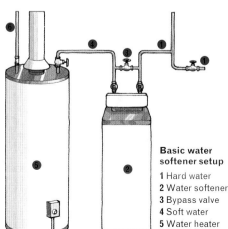

Basic water softener setup

1 Hard water
2 Water softener
3 Bypass valve
4 Soft water
5 Water heater
6 Soft hot water

SOFT WATER TO WATER HEATER

HARD-WATER INLET

HARD WATER TO WATER SOFTENER

Water softener piping
You can make your own 3-way bypass valve for a water softener installation by following this diagram.

Solder risers to water-supply pipes

Water filters

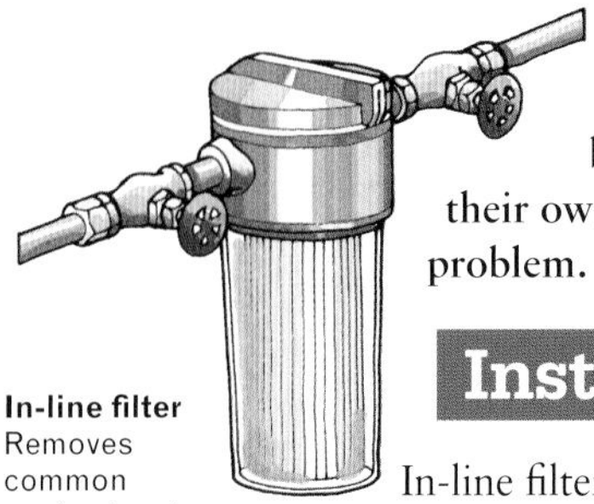

In-line filter Removes common contaminants from home water systems.

The quality of the drinking water in this country is very high, from large cities to small rural towns.But municipal treatment can vary from day to day, and countless private wells have not been tested since they were drilled. For these reasons and others, more people are starting to treat their own drinking water. The good news is that there's an equipment solution for nearly every water problem. The bad news is that no single piece of equipment handles all the problems.

Installing in-line filters

In-line filters are good at removing sediment and organic and inorganic contaminants in gas, liquid, and particle form. Carbon filters are some of the most popular. In-line filters must be installed in a vertical position in the main water line of the house—before the line branches off to any fixtures or appliances.

Begin work by draining the water system. Then cut out a section of pipe (usually about 14 inches long) to accommodate the top of the filter body and two short piping stubs on both sides. Install a male adapter, with a pipe stub soldered in the end, on both sides of the filter. Then install a shutoff valve on both of the stubs so you can turn off the water flow at any time. If you use valves that have a compression fitting on one end, you won't have to solder the stubs to the valves. To maintain electrical grounding for your home, add a jumper cable over the top of the filter.

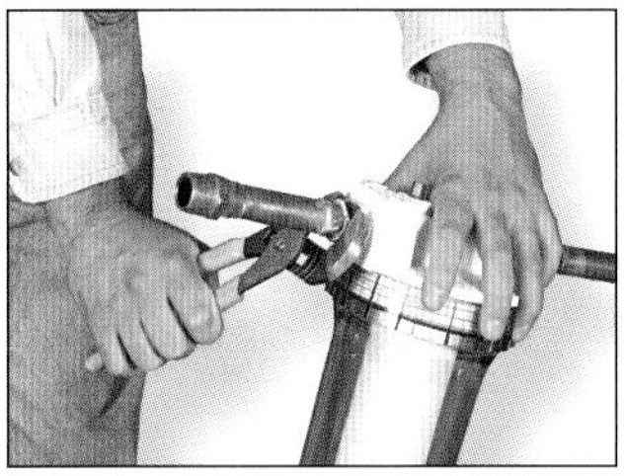

Install adapters with stubs in both sides of filter

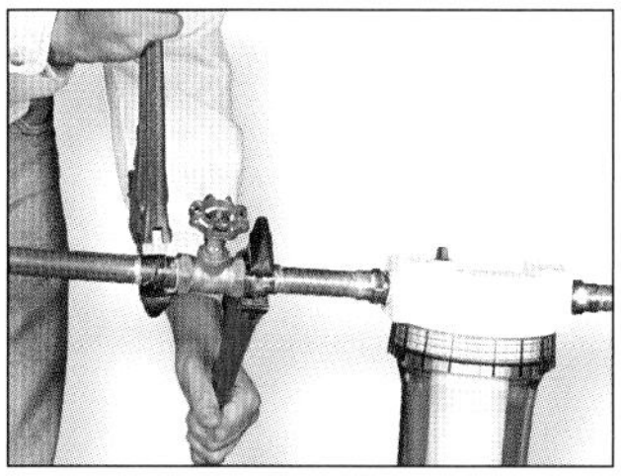

Install shutoff valve on both sides of the filter

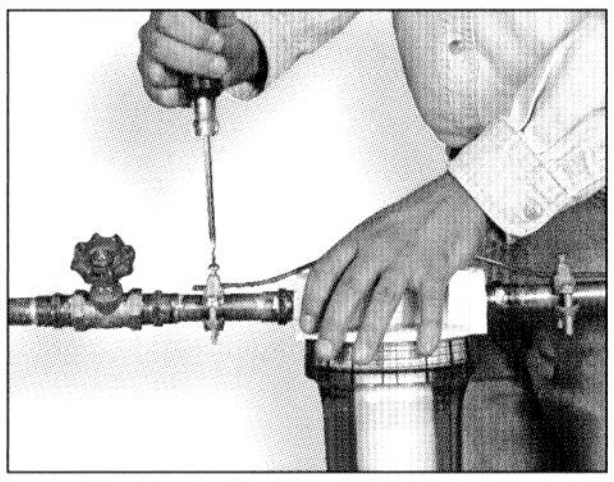

Add jumper wire to maintain electrical grounding

Installing reverse-osmosis filters

Reverse-osmosis (RO) filters are very good at removing nitrates and hazardous chemical pollutants. But they don't remove biological contaminants. If you have both problems, you have to install two filtering systems.

RO units work by forcing water through a permeable membrane that does the filtering. Because this membrane is so dense, the filter can't handle high water volumes. RO units are not designed for complete plumbing system filtration. They're usually installed under kitchen sinks to purify drinking and cooking water.

To install one, first assemble the filter according to the manufacturer's instructions. Then mount it on the inside wall of your kitchen-sink cabinet. Slide the water-storage tank into the cabinet and connect the tank to the filter with the tubing provided.

The unit comes with a countertop-mounted dispensing faucet. It can be installed in the sink, if you remove the spray hose, or on the countertop next to the sink. If you put it on the countertop, you'll have to bore a hole through the counter to mount it. Attach supply tubing from the storage tank to this faucet.

To tap into the household water, install a saddle tap on the cold water supply line that serves the kitchen sink. Then run tubing from the tap to the filter unit.

This filter requires a drain connection to the kitchen-sink waste line. Drill a hole in this pipe and install a drain saddle according to the instructions supplied with the filter. Connect a hose from this saddle to the drain port on the filter.

Turn on the water to the filter and flush at least two full tanks of water through the faucet before using the water for drinking or cooking. This should take a couple of days. Be patient. The kits come with a preservative solution inside that can cause flu-like symptoms unless it is flushed out completely.

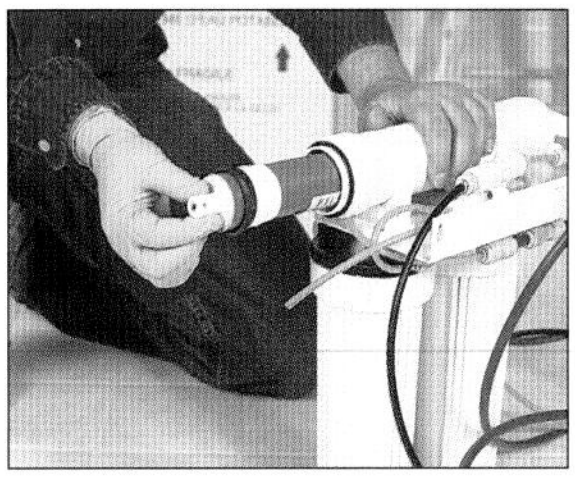

Install filter cartridge

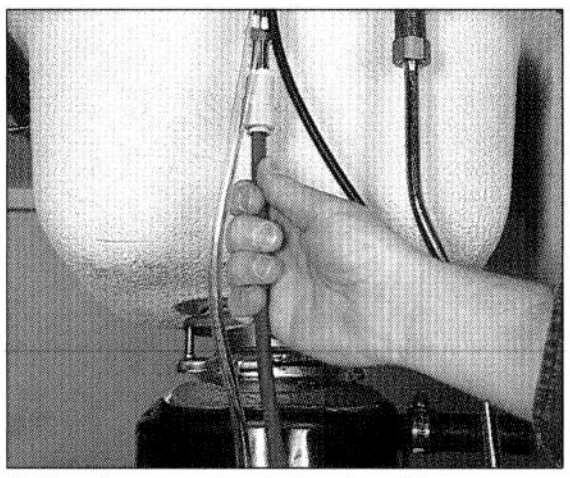

Attach supply tube to dispenser

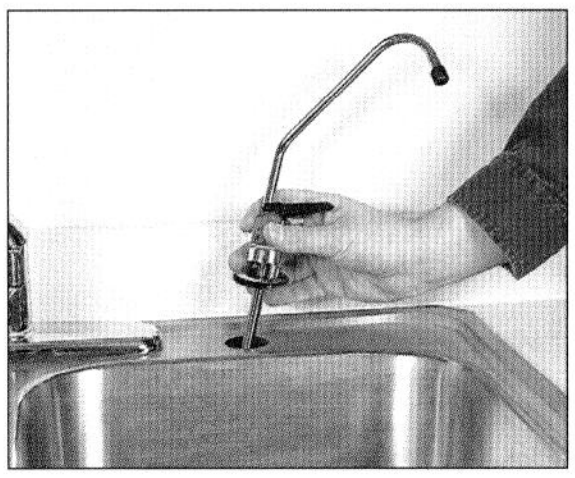

Mount dispenser in sink hole

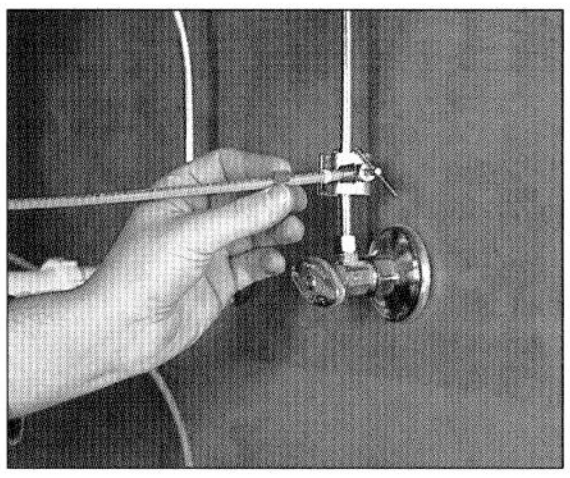

Attach supply tube to saddle valve

Rural septic systems

If a septic system fails it will usually be in the winter or early spring. The reasons are twofold. First, frozen soil releases no water through plant roots and little through evaporation. This means that leach fields in winter are relegated to simple storage troughs, nearly filled with water. Second, spring is often the wettest time of year. These two conditions make for wetter, oxygen-saturated soil around the leach fields, which, in turn, slows or reduces the nitrification of effluent. At some point the leach fields can hold no more water and the system backs up.

To circumvent this, researchers developed a leach field that was built above ground in the shape of a mound. With sufficient ground slope between the tank and the leach field, effluent flows directly into the mound. When the terrain is flat, a pump is used to lift the waste to mound level.

The mound is constructed of a layered aggregate containing a gridwork of perforated pipe. Because sewage is warm when leaving the tank, the mound does not freeze and evaporation occurs through the top as well as through the four sides, even in winter. Mound systems are still new in parts of the country, but most health departments will allow their use.

The most common private waste-disposal system in this country is the septic system. It's composed of two major parts: a septic tank, which stores house waste, and a leach field, which disperses the waste into the ground after it has been broken down in the septic tank. Both of these are buried underground as is the piping that connects them. Raw-sewage cesspools, for obvious reasons, are no longer permitted for residential use. When well maintained, a septic system can last the life of a house. When not maintained, a system can fail in five years. Once it fails, it can't be reclaimed.

How a septic system works

As raw sewage is drained into the septic tank, bacteria break the sewage down into gray water, bottom sludge, and surface scum. As more sewage enters the tank, gray water rises through a baffle and floats out into the leach field. Once in the field, around 60 percent of the gray water is consumed by plants. The remaining 40 percent is lost through surface evaporation. The nitrate residue is then consumed by another kind of bacteria found only in the top 4 feet of soil.

Because of the scum and sludge left in the tank, your septic tank must be pumped out every two or three years. Otherwise, the sludge at the bottom will rise, thus reducing the capacity of the tank. The scum will continue to build up at the top of the tank until it is deep enough to make its way through the baffle and into the leach field. Once inside the leach field, it will coat the walls of the trench and clog the gravel storage area. When the walls of the leach field are sealed, the field will fail.

To keep your septic tank and leach field in working order, have the tank pumped at least once every three to four years and don't plant trees near the tank or on top of the leach field.

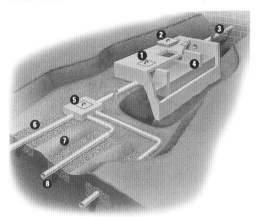

Basic components of a typical septic system
1 Septic tank	**5** Distribution box
2 Access cover	**6** Gravel
3 House sewer pipe	**7** Leach field
4 Baffle	**8** Perforated pipe

Repairing a collapsed culvert leach field

Some leach fields use concrete half-culverts (inverted on concrete blocks) instead of perforated pipe. Culverts can break when a vehicle is driven over them. If a section does collapse, it can be dug up and replaced. (Hire an excavator with a backhoe for this.)

Because leach fields work best near the surface, you will find the top of the culvert only a foot or two down. Dig the dirt above the culvert away and keep it to one side of the ditch. When you hit gravel, dig it out of the trench and store it on the other side.

Each culvert will be 3 to 4 feet long. When you've removed the gravel from around the broken one, pull it out. Clean most of the gravel out of the ditch and set a new length of half culvert on the blocks.

Push the gravel back into the ditch until the culvert's dome is covered. Lay landscape fabric over the gravel and fill the remainder of the ditch with dirt. Because uncompacted dirt will settle in time, leave a 4-inch mound over the trench. Then soak the dirt and replace the sod or plant new grass.

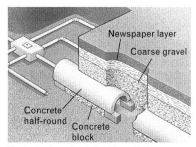

Typical culvert leach field installation

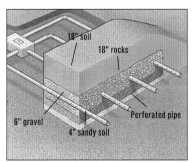

Mound system construction details

Sprinkler systems

With the introduction of plastic pipe and fittings to the plumbing market, simple do-it-yourself sprinkler systems are a lot easier to install, even in cold weather climates. Still, the most difficult aspect of any in-ground sprinkler job is digging all the pipe trenches. If you don't want to make this harder than it already is, plan your layout carefully before you set a spade to the ground.

Installing a system

You will have to make a scale drawing of your lawn and include features such as driveways and sidewalks, which may present piping barriers. You should be able to cover your lawn evenly by matching sprinkler heads to specific areas. Use single-direction pop-up heads for terraces and flower gardens, 45- and 90-degree heads for corners and along drives, and 360-degree heads for open spaces. No matter which combination you use, you will have some overlap. Overlapping patterns are not a real problem because coverage is lighter the farther away from the heads. By researching the products on the market, you can get a good idea of how each head works and in which situation each should be used. You can do the layout yourself or get help from your local dealer.

Joining plastic pipe
Plastic pipe is easily assembled.Use cleaning solvent and rag to prepare joints. Then join parts with solvent cement.

Another important factor in planning your system is the water pressure in your home. With high pressure, and just a few good heads, you may be able to feed all heads from a single line and valve. But, with less pressure and a bigger system, you need to divide the system up into two or three separately controlled lines so that one section can be charged at a time. Most sprinkler dealers will lend you a pressure gauge designed to be used on outside faucets. When testing for water pressure, make sure that none of the indoor fixtures is running at the same time.

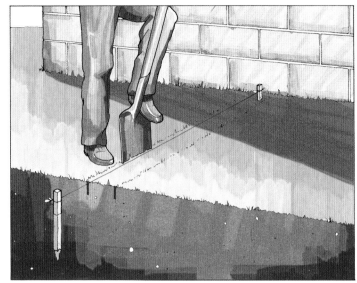

Lay out your trench lines with string, then cut through the sod with a flat-blade shovel or spade

Glue tees into pipe at head locations

Test fit heads to check proper height

Apply **Teflon** tape to fitting before final assembly

Insert drain fittings into drain tees

Place gravel under drains to prevent clogging

Glue piping lines to zone-control valves

Making water connections

With all heads installed, replace the sod all the way up to the house connection. At the house, you will have to bore a hole into the basement to access your water supply. This is best done through a first-floor rim joist. But make the hole wherever it's convenient. You also need to install a vacuum breaker in the water line that goes into the house. (A vacuum breaker is necessary to keep your in-house plumbing from back-siphoning any contaminated water. It also allows your sprinkler heads to drain properly.) Run a copper pipe from the vacuum breaker down to the ground and attach it to the plastic sprinkler pipe with an adapter and an elbow. Use copper pipe on the other side of the breaker to enter the house.

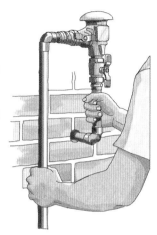

Install vacuum breaker on outside wall of house

Permanent indoor connections

Once the pipe is through the basement wall, you have to join it to a cold water supply line in the house. Choose the one nearest to the hole. Shut off and drain the house water. Then cut the pipe and install a tee in this line. Because the supply line will likely be ¾-inch diameter, you'll have to increase the pipe diameter to the 1-inch size used outdoors. Also install a full flow shutoff valve at this point.

Before you complete the joint between the outside and inside lines, install a boiler drain valve just below where the sprinkler line comes into the house. This valve will help you seasonally drain the system, before winter.

When all the assembly is complete, turn on the water, bleed the air out of the lines, and check for any leaks.

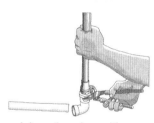

Join system pipes with adapter and elbow

Install tee and shutoff valve in house water line

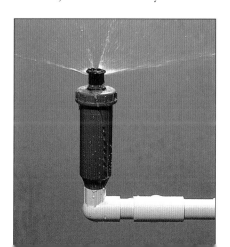

Install tee and a drain valve below exit pipe

Submersible pumps

If you live in a city or a town, you probably don't think much about how water gets to your house. All you need to know is how to open the tap. But if you move a few miles outside of town, this picture could change. Most rural homes have their own wells and must maintain a fairly complicated system that gets water from the ground to the tap.

There are several different systems that accomplish this. One of the most common is the submersible pump system. This consists of a cylindrical pump that is lowered in the casing to the bottom of a deep well. It's connected to a storage tank in the house with plastic pipe. It's also connected to the electric system with waterproof cable. When the pressure switch senses reduced pressure in the storage tank it turns on the pump and more water is delivered.

To keep the system from freezing in northern climates, the pipe that joins the pump and the tank is installed below the local frost line.

The pumps are durable and last a long time. But when they wear out, the well cap is removed and the pump and all the piping is pulled up through the top of the well.

Water-well pressure switch

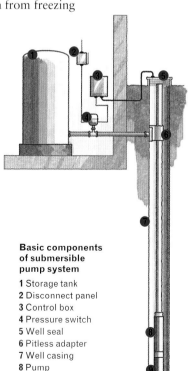

Basic components of submersible pump system

1 Storage tank
2 Disconnect panel
3 Control box
4 Pressure switch
5 Well seal
6 Pitless adapter
7 Well casing
8 Pump
9 Motor

Plumbing outdoors

Seepage pits

Outdoor plumbing can be a welcome alternative to stringing garden hoses across your yard. A freezeless spigot, or hydrant, in your garden is a lot more convenient than a bunch of hoses. A seepage pit to serve a garage workshop drain can also make life easier. Outdoor plumbing is not much more difficult to install than indoor plumbing. The obvious difference is that, in some places, outdoor plumbing has to withstand subzero temperatures.

Freezeless yard hydrants

Attach vacuum-breaker fitting to sillcocks to prevent back-siphoning of polluted water into house supply lines.

Yard hydrants have their shutoff locations buried below frost level. When you lift the handle at the top of the hydrant, you pull a long stem inside the casing upward. The stopper at the lower end of the stem is lifted out of its seat and water travels up through the pipe casing to the spout. When you push the handle down, the stem pushes the stopper back into its seat and interrupts the flow of water. The water left standing in the casing then drains back through an opening at the bottom of the hydrant, just below frost level.

Finished grade
Hydrant
Basement wall
Gravel
Trench   Undisturbed soil

Typical yard hydrant installation. Supply piping is below frost line.

Installing a hydrant

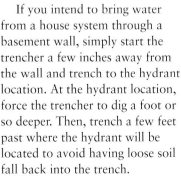

Remove hydrant head to service parts

Lift out valve stem to replace old stopper

Whether you bring water from a basement wall or a buried rural line, you will have to rent a trenching machine. The depth of the trench you dig will be dictated by how deeply the ground freezes in your area. Hydrants can be purchased in several lengths for a variety of conditions. A 5-foot depth is common in colder climates.

If you intend to bring water from a house system through a basement wall, simply start the trencher a few inches away from the wall and trench to the hydrant location. At the hydrant location, force the trencher to dig a foot or so deeper. Then, trench a few feet past where the hydrant will be located to avoid having loose soil fall back into the trench.

With the trench ready, measure carefully and drill directly into the open trench from inside the basement. Then slide one end of a coil of buriable plastic pipe through the wall from the outside and reel the coil out in the trench to the hydrant location. Leave the hydrant end of the coil out of the ditch so that you can attach the brass conversion fitting. Attach this fitting to the supply pipe with stainless-steel hose clamps. Before putting the hydrant in the trench, pour about 50 pounds of gravel into the deeper section of the ditch. This will provide a small reservoir for the drain water from the hydrant. Set the hydrant in place and pour a few more pounds of gravel around the hydrant. Then backfill the trench and make the connection to a convenient supply line inside the house.

Seepage pits are miniature leach fields designed to dispose of gray water discharged from remote floor drains. If your drainage system is served by a municipal sewer, seepage pits will not be needed, and, in most cases, not allowed. If, however, your home is in a rural area, a seepage pit can save you the trouble of tapping into your septic system when outbuildings are some distance from the house.

The size of the pit you build will depend upon anticipated volume. For a garage or workshop, a 3- or 4-foot inside diameter is often sufficient. Before starting the job, however, check with local code authorities for structural guidelines.

Begin by digging a more or less round pit roughly 5 feet deep and 5 feet in diameter. Then lay a starter course of concrete blocks side by side around the outside walls of the pit. Follow with a series of courses until you are within 1½ feet of the finished grade. At this point, you can trench the drainage pipe to the pit. If you slide the drainpipe through an opening in one of the top blocks, it will be held permanently in place. Finally, construct a cover from treated lumber.

In sandy soil, tape a few layers of newspaper around the outside perimeter of the block to keep the soil from sifting in when you backfill. The newspaper will decompose after the soil settles. Regrade the ground and plant some grass.

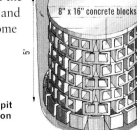

5'
Wood cover
8" x 16" concrete blocks
5'

Typical seepage pit installation details

Open fires

For centuries open fires were our only domestic heating. Inefficient and wasteful, their only benefits were the radiant heat from the burning fuel and some milder warmth from heated chimneys. They are nowadays used mainly as attractive focal points in homes heated by more modern means.

How an open fire works

To burn well, any fire needs a good supply of oxygen **(1)** and a means for smoke and gases to escape **(2)**. If either is cut off, the fire will be stifled and eventually go out.

The domestic open fire is built on a barred grate **(3)** through which ash and debris fall and oxygen is sucked up into the base of the fire to maintain combustion.

As the fuel burns, it gives off heated gases which expand and become lighter than the ambient air so that they rise **(4)**. To prevent the gases and smoke from drifting out and filling the room, a chimney above the fire gives them an escape route, taking them above the roof level of the house to be discharged in the outside air.

As the hot gases rise, they cause suction at the bottom of the fire that draws in a supply of oxygen to keep it burning. For this reason, a good fire needs not only an effective chimney but also good ventilation in the room where it is burning, so that the air consumed by the fire can be continually replenished.

In modern homes or older homes with new, tightly sealed doors and windows, a fire may not burn properly due to a lack of consistent air supply. In these cases, extra ventilation must be provided—either through a dedicated fireplace vent or by simply opening a window slightly to admit the necessary air.

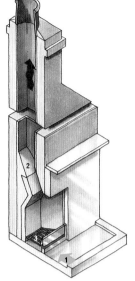

Oxygen in, smoke out
1 Air is sucked in as the smoke rises.
2 Smoke escapes up the narrow flue.
3 The grate lets air in and allows ash to collect underneath.
4 Smoke and gases are vented to the outside.

Sweeping chimneys

All solid fuels give off dust, ash, acids, and tarry substances as they burn, and this material is carried up through the chimney, where a part of it condenses and collects as a substance called creosote. If too much creosote collects in a chimney, it not only reduces the gas flow (and prevents the fire from burning properly) it can even cause a blockage. More importantly, the creosote can ignite, causing a potentially dangerous chimney fire.

To prevent creosote buildup, clean your chimney at least once a year before the heating season. It may be necessary to clean the chimney again during the heating season—especially if an efficient, airtight wood stove is in use or green wood has been burned. It's a good idea to have your chimney inspected by a professional chimney sweep, as well.

Though it's a dirty job, you can clean a chimney without making a great deal of mess to be cleaned up afterward, provided you take some care. You can rent the brushes, but be sure to get a size that matches your chimney. (It should fit tightly.) Modern ones have nylon bristles and fiberglass extension rods.

Remove all loose items from the fireplace surround and hearth, then roll back the carpet and cover it with a drop cloth or newspapers for protection. Drape a large old sheet or blanket over the surround, weighting it down along the top and leaning something heavy against each side to form a seal with the edges.

Actual cleaning may be done by pushing a brush up from a fireplace or by forcing it down from the chimney top. If the roof is dangerous or the chimney is covered by a chimney cap, sweep from inside the house. (You may have to remove the damper plate at the base of the flue to fit the brushes in.) If possible, sweep from the top down. To do this, first be sure the fireplace opening is tightly covered with drop cloths. From the roof, insert the brush into the chimney and push it down toward the fireplace opening. Thread on additional rods as required to reach the proper depth, and work the brushes up and down. When you reach the bottom, withdraw the brush. Wait 1 hour for the dust to settle, then vacuum the debris from the fireplace floor using a heavy-duty industrial vacuum cleaner available from rental centers.

Though using a brush is a time-honored and effective way of sweeping a chimney, in recent years other methods have been found to help with this dirty job (see right).

Cleaning from above
Insert brush and rods at chimney top. Brush up and down, threading on additional rods as required.

Sweeping a chimney
Seal off the fireplace with an old sheet and feed the brush rods up under it.

● **Vacuum sweeping**
You can have a chimney cleaned with a special vacuum cleaner. Its nozzle, inserted through a cover over the fire opening, sucks the soot out of the chimney. Although this is a relatively clean method, it may not remove heavy soot deposits or other obstructions.

● **Chemical cleaning**
There are chemicals that will remove light deposits and help prevent a buildup in the future. In liquid or powder form, they are sprinkled onto a hot fire, producing a nontoxic gas that causes soot to crumble away from inside the chimney. Keep in mind, though, that a thorough cleaning by brush is considered the best approach.

49

Curing a smoky fireplace

Regulating draft
Regulate chimney draft by adjusting damper. Operate adjusting arm using poker when fire is burning.

A well-functioning fireplace is the product of many design elements. When fireplace smoke drifts into the room, rather than escaping up the chimney, there may be several causes. If the fireplace has always been a smoky one, chances are that its construction includes one or more design flaws. If the condition is a recent development, solving the problem may require only a simple adjustment or cleaning.

Remedying simple problems

If the fireplace smokes only occasionally or has just begun to smoke, run through this checklist of minor adjustments. First, be certain that when the fire is burning, the damper is fully open.

Most dampers can be adjusted when hot by pushing the protruding end of the handle with a poker. Check, too, that the chimney is free of obstructions, especially if a normally clean-burning fireplace suddenly starts smoking. Along with this, make sure that the chimney is regularly cleaned. Accumulated soot and creosote can eventually cause smoking and, worse, a chimney fire.

Check that the fire is built well back in the firebox so that no burning logs project beyond the fireplace opening. Try raising the height of the fire several inches by placing the logs on a grate elevated on firebricks. Inadequate intake of air—too little to support combustion or feed the chimney's draft—may also be the culprit, especially if you have altered the ventilation pattern in the room by adding insulation and weather stripping. To alleviate this cause of a smoky fireplace, open a door or window to admit more air.

Correcting chimney faults

To produce an updraft, air must flow steadily across the opening at the top of a chimney. This creates a partial vacuum within, which aids in drawing the heated air from the fireplace. In order for the air to be unobstructed as it flows, a chimney must be at least 3 feet higher than any object within a 10-foot radius, including roof peaks, trees, television antennas, or other chimneys. If you cannot increase the height of a too-short chimney by adding to it, attaching a chimney cap or smoke puller (a fan mounted in the chimney opening) may help. Before under-taking such modifications, consult a professional chimney sweep or mason.

Uncapped chimneys should have a sloping cowl of mortar on all four sides to direct passing air up and over the opening. Otherwise, air striking the chimney will eddy and swirl erratically, which may cause an uneven flow of air from the fireplace.

COWL
3'   10'

Correcting fireplace proportions

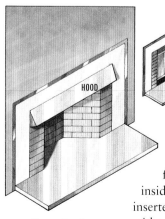

Remedies for smoky fireplaces
A hood or glass doors can prevent smoke from entering a room.

HOOD

GLASS DOORS

To draw smoke upward properly, the dimensions of the chimney flue must bear a certain proportional relationship to those of the brick-lined or steel-lined area where the fire is actually built (called the firebox). Also, the firebox itself must be built to a certain shape in order to both reflect heat outward and direct smoke upward. Often, either the firebox is built too large for the flue rising inside the chimney or the flue (usually a retrofit inserted into a chimney that was originally built without one) is too small.

One solution is to fit a metal fireplace hood, available from fireplace and woodstove supply stores and some home centers, across the top of the fireplace opening to decrease its overall size and also to smoke that might otherwise seep out. To install the hood, first determine how large it must be by holding a piece of metal or dampened plywood across the top of the fireplace when a fire is burning. As the fireplace begins to smoke, gradually lower the sheet of material until the smoking is contained. Buy a hood this size. Most hoods attach to the fireplace surround by means of special masonry hangers.

Another solution is to fit glass doors across the entire front opening of the fireplace. These, too, are available in many sizes from fireplace and woodstove stores, as well as home centers. Although some heat may be lost to the room when the doors are closed, the fire is entirely enclosed and smoke is completely contained. There are also energy-efficient models that actually enhance the amount of heat produced by the fireplace.

Removing a fireplace

To take out an antique fire surround and hearth is easy enough, but it can create alot of dust and debris. Any hammering is likely to cause quantities of soot to fall down the chimney. Before you start, clean the chimney, move all furniture away from the fireplace, roll back the carpet, and cover everything with drop cloths. There is a good demand for Victorian fire surrounds, and some are valuable. If you remove yours undamaged, you may be able to sell it.

Removing the hearth

Most old-fashioned hearths were laid after the fire surround had been fitted, and so must come out first. But, check beforehand that your surround has not been installed on top of the hearth.

Wear safety goggles and heavy gloves against flying debris, and use a 2-pound sledgehammer and a bricklayer's chisel to break the mortar bond between the hearth and the subhearth below.

Knocking in wood wedges will help. Lever the hearth free with a crowbar or the blade of a strong garden spade and lift it clear. It will be heavy, so get someone to help.

Some older hearths are laid level with the surrounding floorboards and have a layer of tiles on top of them. Here, all that's needed is to lift the tiles off carefully with a bricklayer's chisel.

Removing the surround

Most fire surrounds are held to the wall by screws that are driven through metal lugs set around their edges. They will be concealed by the plaster on the chimney. To find the lugs, chip away a 1-inch strip of plaster around the surround, then expose the lugs completely and take out the screws. If they are rusted and immovable, soak them in penetrating oil, leave for a few hours, and try again. If that fails, drill out their heads. The surround will be heavy, so have some help available when you lever it from the wall and lower it carefully onto the floor.

Brick and stone surrounds
A brick or stone surround can be removed a piece at a time, using a bricklayer's chisel to break the mortar joints. There may also be metal ties holding it to the wall.

Marble surrounds
Marble surrounds are made in sections, so remove the shelf first, then the frieze or lintel, and last, the side jambs.

Wooden surrounds
A wooden surround will probably be held by screws driven through its sides and top into strips that are fixed to the chimney inside the surround. The screwheads will be hidden by wooden plugs or filler. Chisel these out, remove the screws, and lift away the surround.

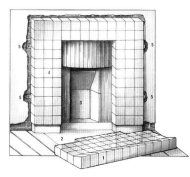

Taking out a tiled fireplace
1 Superimposed hearth pulled away
2 Constructional hearth at floor level
3 Fireback
4 Fire surround
5 Metal lugs hold many surrounds in place

Replacing cracked tiles

Cracked or broken tiles in a hearth or fire surround should be replaced with new ones, but you may not be able to match those in an old fireplace. One solution here is to buy some new tiles that pleasantly complement or contrast with the originals and replace more than just the damaged one or two, making a random or symmetrical pattern.

Break out the damaged tile with a hammer and cold chisel, working from the center of the tile outward. Wear thick gloves and safety goggles, and protect nearby surfaces with drop cloths. When the tile is out, remove all traces of old adhesive or mortar and vacuum up the dust.

If necessary, cut the new tile to shape. Spread heat-resistant tile adhesive thickly on its back and on the surface where it is to go. Don't get adhesive on its edges or on the edges of surrounding tiles. Set the tile in place, taking care that the clearance is equal all around, and wipe off any excess adhesive. Leave it to set and then apply grout.

If you are replacing only one tile, it's not worth buying a large quantity of adhesive. Instead, mix a paste from coarse sawdust and wood glue, which will work just as well. If the tile is very close to the fire, you can use some fire cement.

Complete retiling
If a lot of the tiles are damaged or crazed, your best option may be to retile the entire surround and hearth. This is much less trouble than it sounds, as you can simply stick the new tiles directly on top of the old ones. First make sure that the old tiles are clean and remove any loose pieces, then apply your tile adhesive and stick the tiles on in the ordinary way.

Cast-iron fireplace
Some old fireplace surrounds are in demand. Paint can be stripped from cast-iron surrounds, as shown above.

● **Saving a surround**
Fire surrounds can be very heavy, especially stone, slate, or marble ones. If you wish to keep yours intact for sale, lay an old mattress in front of it before you pull it from the wall so it will be less likely to break if it should fall.

Chipping out a damaged tile
Start in the middle and work out to the edges. Clean out all old mortar or adhesive.

Sealing a fireplace opening

Installing an old-fashioned fireplace

If you have removed an old fireplace, you can close the opening by bricking it up or by covering it with drywall. The latter will make it easier to reinstall the fireplace at a later date. In either case, fit a ventilator in the opening just above the baseboard. The airflow through the chimney will prevent condensation from forming and seeping through the brickwork to damage wall decorations.

Restoring the floor

If the floor is solid, you need only bring the subhearth up level with it, using cement. You can also do this with a wood floor, if it is to be carpeted. If you want exposed floorboards, the subhearth will have to be broken away with a hammer and cold chisel to make room for new floor framing and floorboards.

Sealing the opening with bricks

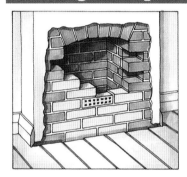

If you wish to brick up the firebox opening, remove bricks from alternate courses at the edges of the opening so that the new brickwork can be "toothed in." Provide ventilation for the chimney by fitting a brick vent in the center of the brickwork and just above baseboard level. Plaster the brickwork and allow it to dry out thoroughly before you redecorate the wall. Finally, lever the old pieces of baseboard from the ends of the fireplace and replace them with a full-length piece from corner to corner.

Sealing the opening with drywall

Cut a panel from ½-inch drywall and nail it onto a wood frame mounted inside the fire opening. Use 2 x 4 lumber for the frame. Nail it into the opening with masonry nails, setting it in so that when the drywall is nailed on, it will lie flush with the surrounding wall if it is to be papered or painted to match the other walls in the room. Place the frame ⅛ inch deeper if you plan to add a plaster skim coat to the surface of the drywall. After decorating or plastering the panel, fit a ventilator in the center as shown below.

An inset frame to support plasterboard

An unused chimney must be ventilated

Closing the chimney top

Commercial cowl

Half-round ridge tile

When you close off a fireplace opening, you will have to cap the chimney in such a way as to keep rain out while allowing the air from the vent in the room to escape. Use a half-round ridge tile bedded in cement or a metal cowl, either of which will do the job.

In the past 30 years or so, traditional fireplaces have vanished from many older houses, swept away in the name of modernization. But now they are being appreciated again and even sought after. You can install an old-fashioned fireplace with simple tools and a few weekends of work.

Most period fire surrounds are held in place by lugs screwed to the wall, but some can be attached with mortar. A plaster surround can be held with dabs of bonding plaster.

First, remove a strip of plaster from around the fire opening, about 2 inches wider all around than the surround.

If the surround incorporates a cast-iron centerpiece, it must be fitted first. Most of them simply stand on the back hearth, but some have lugs for screwing to the wall. If yours has lugs, use metal wall plugs or expansion bolts. Fit lengths of fiberglass-rope packing where the grate or centerpiece touches the fireback.

Hold the surround in place, mark the wall for the screw holes, and drill them. Use a level to check that the surround is upright and the mantel horizontal, and make any needed corrections by fitting wooden wedges behind the surround or bending the lugs backward or forward.

An alternative method for plaster surrounds is to apply mortar or plaster to the wall and prop the surround against it with boards until the mortar or plaster sets.

Replace the hearth or build a new one. Set the hearth on dabs of mortar and point around the edges with the same material.

Replaster the wall and fit new baseboard molding between the hearth and the corners of the chimney masonry.

Enclosed fireplaces

A modern enclosed fireplace, or room heater, can be freestanding or inset. Both are very efficient at heating individual rooms and can help offset the cost of conventional central heating. The toughened-glass doors of closed fireplaces and insets allow the glow of the fire to be seen, and they open to allow extra fuel to be added.

A freestanding heater on the hearth

Freestanding room heaters are designed to stand on the hearth, forward of the chimney masonry. They radiate extra warmth from their surfaces, but their size can make them obtrusive in small rooms. You may also have to extend the hearth as required by your local building code.

A heater of this type has a flue outlet at its rear which is connected to the chimney, and the easiest way of arranging this is to run the stovepipe into a metal backplate that closes off the fire opening. The projecting end of the outlet must be at least 4 inches from the back wall of the firebox.

The closure plate should be an appropriate fireproof panel—check with a woodstove supply store to find the latest type available. Use metal wall anchors to hold the screws, and seal the joint between the plate and the opening with fiberglass rope and heat-resistant cement.

Alternatively, stovepipes for freestanding heaters can be fitted into the fireplace damper opening after removing the damper plate.

1 A backplate closes off fire opening

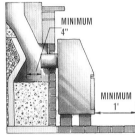

2 Important measurements for room heater

An inset room heater

An inset room heater has its flue outlet mounted on top, to be connected to a chimney closure plate or stovepipe rising through the chimney.

This type of appliance is designed to fill and seal the fire opening completely, so to install one you may have to modify your present fireplace surround or even, if the opening is very large, build a new one. The sides of the surround must be exactly at right angles to the hearth, as the front portion of the heater's casing has to be sealed to both. If the surround and the hearth form an odd angle, a good seal with the heater casing will be impossible. The seal can be made with fiberglass-rope packing material.

More often, inset room heaters are screwed down to the firebox floor, and some may need a vermiculite-based infill around the back of the casing that must be in place before the chimney closure plate is fitted and the flue outlet connected.

Some come supplied with their own fire surrounds, complete with drop-in closure plates designed to make their installation easier. Finish the job by restoring the fireplace brickwork, and replaster if necessary.

A freestanding heater in the fireplace

Some freestanding room heaters are designed to stand in the fire opening. This type of heater has a flue outlet in its top that must be connected to a closure plate set in the base of the chimney.

The plate can be metal or precast concrete. To make room enough to fit it, remove some bricks from the chimney masonry just above the opening but below the load-bearing lintel. If the plate is concrete, take out a course of bricks around the bottom of the chimney to support it properly.

You can insert a metal plate into a cleared-out mortar joint or fasten it with expansion bolts. Bed the plate on heat-resistant cement, sealing the edges above and below. Check that the heater's outlet enters the chimney flue, and seal the plate joint with fiberglass rope and an appropriate cement.

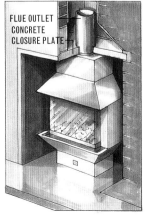

A horizontal plate seals off chimney

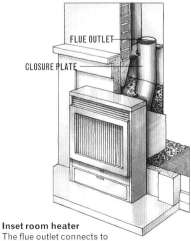

Inset room heater
The flue outlet connects to a horizontal closure plate in the base of the chimney. Some heaters require an infill behind the casing.

Wood-burning stoves

Choosing a flue liner

Wood-burning stoves
Available in a range of traditional designs, wood-burning stoves epitomize country living.

One of the most economical ways to keep a room warm is by means of a modern, slow-combustion wood-burning stove—if you have access to cheap wood. Like fireplace inserts or inset room heaters, they can be stood on the hearth with rear flue outlets or installed in the fireplace with top-mounted outlets. A good wood-burning stove can burn all day or night on one load of wood.

If a wood-burning stove is installed in place of a fireplace, it's best placed forward of the masonry so that you get the full benefit of the heat that radiates from its surfaces. You can stand it on an existing hearth, provided that the hearth projects the required minimum as indicated by your local building code or the literature that came with the stove. Otherwise, you will have to construct an appropriate fireproof base. Again, your building office will have guidelines and requirements. Common materials for this job are stone, brick, or tile.

A wood-burning stove can be connected to a stainless-steel, insulated flue and this can be passed through a vertical back closure plate that seals off an existing fireplace opening, or through a horizontal plate that closes off the base of the chimney.

More commonly, the stovepipe connects to a masonry chimney through a metal fitting called a thimble that's installed in the brickwork. Ventilated thimbles and fiberglass packing are used for passage through walls when there is no other option for installation.

If an insulated, stainless-steel flue is used, make sure the stovepipe connects through a T-fitting so the bottom extension of the fitting can be removed for cleaning.

It's important to follow local fire codes and building regulations when installing a woodstove. These generally include setting the unit at a safe distance from combustibles, making a positive connection between the stovepipe and flue, and being sure the flue extends at least 36 inches above the roof.

A flue liner will keep the corrosive elements in smoke from damaging a chimney's brick and mortar. It will also reduce the size of the flue, speeding up the flow of gases and preventing their cooling and condensing. The draft of air through the flue will improve, and the fire will burn more efficiently.

It is important to choose the type of liner appropriate to the kind of heating appliance being used and to be sure it is large enough to keep the fireplace from smoking. Consult the stove dealer or building inspector. Linings are tubes, one-piece or in sections, of metal or other rigid, noncombustible material.

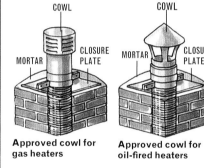

Approved cowl for gas heaters   **Approved cowl for oil-fired heaters**

Safe access

You can rent easy-to-use, light-alloy roof scaffolding. Two units will make a half platform for a central or side chimney; four will provide an all-around platform.

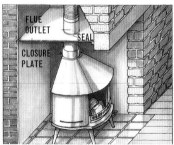

Vertical flue outlet
This type of stove has its flue sealed into the opening of a horizontal closure plate in the base of the chimney.

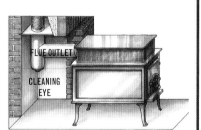

Rear flue outlet
A rear flue outlet allows the stove to stand clear of the fireplace.

Scaffolding is essential for safe working

If your house was built before World War II, its chimney is probably unlined, and is simply a rectangular duct whose brickwork is either stuccoed with cement or exposed. Over the years, corrosive elements in the rising combustion gases eat into the chimney's mortar and brickwork and weaken it, allowing condensation to pass through and form damp patches on the outside and, in extreme cases, letting smoke seep through. This is particularly true where coal or woodburning appliances are in use.

Installing a one-piece flue liner

A popular type of liner is a one-piece, flexible, corrugated tube of stainless steel that is easily fed into a chimney that has bends in it. Unfortunately, this type of liner is not suitable for use with coal or wood-burning appliances. To install it you must get onto the roof and erect scaffolding around the chimney (see below left).

First sweep the chimney, then chop away the mortar around the base of the chimney pot, if installed, with a hammer and cold chisel. Carefully remove the pot—it will be heavy—and lower it to the ground on a rope. Clean up the top of the chimney to expose the brickwork.

The liner is fed into the chimney from the top. Drop a strong weighted line down the chimney **(1)** and attach its other end to the conical end piece of the flue liner. Have an assistant pull gently on the line from below while you feed the liner down into the chimney **(2)**. When the conical end piece emerges below, remove it and connect the liner to a closure plate set across the base of the chimney, or to the flue outlet of the heating appliance. Seal the joint with fiberglass packing and some appropriate cement.

Return to the roof, fit the top closure plate, and bed it in mortar laid on the top of the chimney, adding extra mortar to match the original **(3)**. Finally, fit a cowl to the top of the liner—choose one appropriate to the heating appliance being used (see opposite).

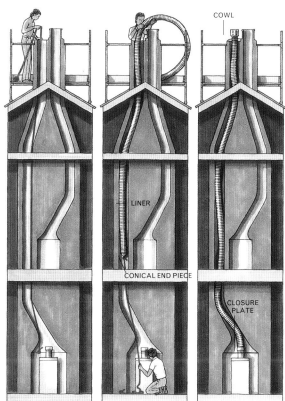

1 Lower weighted line

2 Feed liner down to helper

COWL
LINER
CONICAL END PIECE
CLOSURE PLATE

3 Completed top closure

Because a sectional flue liner has the space around it filled with a lightweight concrete that strengthens and insulates the chimney, it needs a good foundation for the added weight. Like the one-piece liner, it is inserted from the top. This is a complicated job. Consult a professional before you decide to tackle it yourslf.

First, cement a steel baseplate across the bottom of the chimney. Tie the first flue section to a rope and lower it into the chimney. Connect the next section to it by one of the supplied steel collars and lower the two farther down. Continue adding sections and lowering the liner until it reaches the baseplate, then seal it in place.

If there are any bends in the chimney, you will have to break into it at those points to feed the sections in. This may be a job for a professional.

To fill in the chimney around the liner, use concrete made with a lightweight aggregate such as expanded clay or vermiculite. Pour this into the chimney around the liner and finish off the mortar cap at the top.

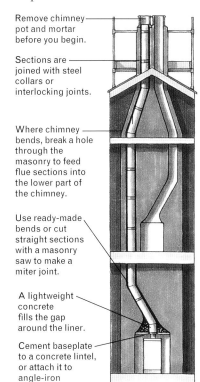

Remove chimney pot and mortar before you begin.

Sections are joined with steel collars or interlocking joints.

Where chimney bends, break a hole through the masonry to feed flue sections into the lower part of the chimney.

Use ready-made bends or cut straight sections with a masonry saw to make a miter joint.

A lightweight concrete fills the gap around the liner.

Cement baseplate to a concrete lintel, or attach it to angle-iron supports.

Casting a flue liner
Professional installers can cast a flue liner in your unlined chimney. A deflated tube is lowered into the chimney. It is inflated, and a lightweight semiliquid mixture is poured into the gap between the tube and the flue. When the mixture has set, the tube is deflated and removed, leaving a smooth-bore flue liner.

Central heating systems

A central heating system supplies heat from a single source to selected rooms, or to all rooms, in the house. It is much more efficient than having an individual heater in each room, as there is only one appliance to be controlled, cleaned, and maintained.

Types of heating systems

Central heating systems are categorized by the medium used to deliver the heat from its source to the various outlets around the house. The three most common systems are forced-air, circulating hot water, and steam. Heat sources for these are normally a gas- or oil-fired furnace (though in some areas coal-fueled and even wood-fueled systems are used), which in turn heats either water in a boiler or air passing through a heat exchanger. Electric heating systems, which derive heat through simple resistance wiring, or which feed heated air through a blower, are less popular systems, due to expensive energy costs. Their advantages, however, are cleanliness and high efficiency.

Forced-air systems

Modern forced-air heating systems consist of a furnace that heats air, a large squirrel-cage blower that circulates that air, and a system of air ducts through which the heated air is directed throughout the house. A secondary system of ducts is also part of the system. Through it, cool air returns to the furnace.

Because of the size and unwieldy nature of the air ducts, forced hot-air heating systems are almost always installed during new construction. From the main duct that leads away from the blower chamber, the delivery ducts branch off, running between floor joists and wall studs to their openings at registers located in outside walls or in the floor near them. Cool air returns through larger, centrally located ducts in the floor. Since hot air rises and cold air falls, the warm air rising along the outside walls heats the rooms, then circulates and cools on the way to the return ducts. This creates a convection current that serves the entire enclosed area.

In large systems, the ductwork is configured to create heating zones—groups of rooms served by a single branch of the system that can be isolated from the rest. By the use of dampers, which physically close off key ducts (dampers are operated manually or by thermostats), the amount of heat directed throughout the house can be economically adjusted so that unused rooms receive less heat.

Typical gas-fired forced-air heating system

1 Furnace (gas)	**6** Warm-air registers
2 Motor	
3 Blower	**7** Cold-air registers
4 Cold-air return	**8** Exhaust (to chimney)
5 Warm-air delivery	

Adjusting the air flowing through a forced-air heating system—a process called balancing—assures that each room receives just the right amount of heat. While the individual registers at the ends of each duct can be manually adjusted or shut, a better system utilizes strategically located dampers mounted inside the ductwork.

Dampers are controlled by means of a handle on the outside of the duct. Turning the handle so it's parallel with the run of the duct allows maximum airflow. Turning it the other way reduces airflow. To balance the system, adjust the dampers until the appropriate settings are achieved. The process is simple but, because each room requires 6 to 8 hours to become properly heated, takes time. Balance the system during a cold spell, when the furnace is running at its peak. Begin by closing down the damper to the most uncomfortably hot area nearest the furnace. This will send greater amounts of heat to more distant registers. After waiting the required heating-up time, move on to the next hot area and adjust the damper there. You can judge the temperature by how the room feels or by holding a thermometer a few feet above the floor.

After you've adjusted all the dampers once (a process that may have taken a week or more), go back and make minor adjustments to any areas that seem too warm or cool. When you're finished, mark the damper handle positions on the ductwork so that they are permanently recorded.

If, after balancing, areas at the far end of duct runs are still too cool, a common solution is to increase the speed of the squirrel-cage blower. This is done by adjusting or replacing one of the drive pulleys on the motor. However, since increasing blower speed places additional strain on the motor, consult a furnace service technician before making the change.

Circulating hot water

The most popular form of central heating is a circulating hot-water system. Water is heated to between 120° and 180°F in a furnace-fired boiler and then is forced by one or more circulator pumps through a system of pipes leading to and from radiators or convectors located throughout the house. Some layouts pump water through a single loop of pipe, off of which branch piping both feeds hot water and returns cooled water to each radiator in sequence. With these systems, careful balancing (as for forced-air systems) is necessary to assure that radiators at the far end of the pipe loop obtain sufficient heat. A better type of layout is one made up of two sets of pipe runs, one to carry only the hot water and one to return only the cooled. These systems require far less adjustment, since water flowing to the farthest radiator does not become mixed with cooled water returning from radiators along the way. Hot-water systems usually include an expansion tank, which contains air, located near the boiler. As water in the system becomes heated and expands, the air in the tank is compressed. This places the water in the system under pressure and prevents it from becoming steam.

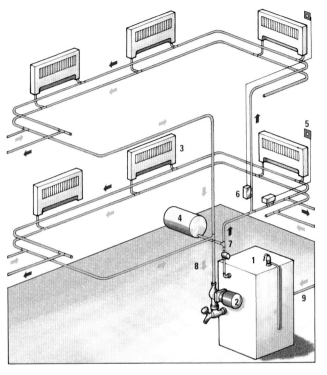

Hot-water system
The water heated by the boiler (**1**) is driven by a circulator pump (**2**) through a two-pipe system to radiators or convector heaters (**3**), which give off heat as the hot water flows through them, gradually warming the rooms to the required temperature. The water then returns to the boiler to be reheated. An expansion tank (**4**) handles the excess volume of water created by heating. Thermostats (**5**) regulate the heat delivered to specific zones in the house by triggering control valves (**6**) or multiple circulators. In the diagram, red indicates the flow of hot water from the boiler (**7**) and blue shows the return flow (**8**). Water is supplied by the household plumbing system (**9**).

Steam heat

Few contemporary homes are built with steam heating systems. However, they are still to be found in many older homes, especially those built prior to World War II. Steam systems operate much like a single-pipe, circulating hot-water system (see above). Water, heated in a boiler until it becomes steam travels under its own pressure through a single pipe a loop around the house. From this pipe, branch lines serve the radiators. As the steam cools by giving up its heat to the radiators, it changes back to water and returns to the boiler by gravity through the same pipe that delivered the steam. Steam systems require neither a circulator nor an expansion tank. Piping must, however, slope downward from all points toward the boiler, and balancing is necessary to properly distribute steam to each room. In addition, steam radiators must be frequently drained of both air and water to remain in working order.

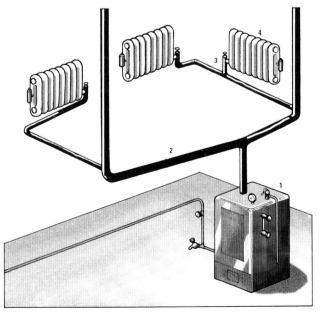

Steam systems
In a single-pipe steam system, steam moves from the boiler (**1**) around the perimeter \of the house through a single pipe that forms a loop (**2**). Flow and return pipes (**3**) divert the steam to each radiator (**4**). From the radiator, the heat moves to the objects in the room and the steam condenses. The water then flows back through the pipes to the boiler. Larger radiators may be required at the end of the loop in order \to compensate for heat loss.

Fuel-burning furnaces

The furnace is the heart of any heating system, whether forced-air, circulating hot water, or steam. Most household furnaces today are heated by gas or oil. To operate properly and efficiently, these furnaces require regular adjustment and periodic care. If carefully maintained, however, modern furnaces are economical heat producers and will provide years of dependable service, often equal to the life of the house. Here are the basics for understanding how typical systems work.

Oil burners

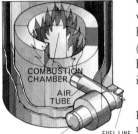

Pressure burner

Vaporizing burner

Oil burners spray fuel oil into a combustion chamber where the oil/air mixture is then ignited to produce heat. The most popular burner design is the pressure (gun) type. Another type, called a vaporizing or pot burner, is less common, but you may find it in older installations or where a smaller heat output is required.

In a high-pressure oil burner, a fine spray of oil is pumped under pressure through a nozzle. Here, it mixes with air and is ignited by a high-voltage electric spark derived from a transformer that's supplied with household current. Low-pressure burners are somewhat similar, the difference being that the oil and air are mixed before exiting the nozzle and pumped into the combustion chamber under far less pressure and through a much larger opening.

Vaporizing burners do not operate under pressure. The combustion area consists of an enclosed shallow pan into which oil is admitted by regulating a manually operated valve. The oil in the pan is ignited by hand, or by a simple electric igniter. The heat from the burning oil causes more oil to vaporize and

combine with air, to burn in the combustion chamber. Air is brought to the combustion chamber by either natural draft or a blower. Because vaporizing oil burners are compact and make very little noise, they are sometimes installed in kitchens or utility rooms. Pressure-type oil burners, on the other hand, are nearly always installed in basements. Vaporizing burners require a finer grade of oil to operate.

Parts of an oil furnace
1 Motor/blower
2 Combustion chamber
3 Heat exchanger
4 Chimney vent
5 On/off switch
6 Combination gauge

**Typical oil burner
(shown equipped for
circulating hot water)**

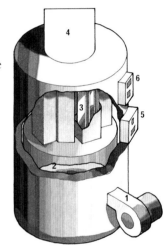

Gas burners

Gas burners are far simpler than oil burners and, since gas itself burns much more cleanly than fuel oil, require less regular maintenance. Still, they should be cleaned and serviced at least every two or three years.

Whether supplied by natural gas or liquefied petroleum (LP gas), furnaces of this type consist merely of a burner assembly and a gas-regulating valve. The burners may be of a type that spread their flame over a large area, or they may merely have multiple openings (or jets), as on a gas kitchen range.

For safety, gas burners incorporate a thermocouple device that shuts off the gas-supply valve when no heat is detected in the combustion area. Should the odor of gas ever be detected near a gas burner, immediately open windows, extinguish any open flames or cigarettes, then leave the house and telephone your gas

or utility company. To avoid generating a small spark that may be enough to ignite escaping gas do not touch electrical switches.

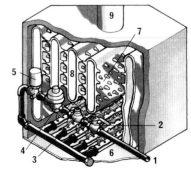

**Parts of a gas
furnace**
1 Gas supply
2 Manual shutoff valve
3 Thermocouple
4 Pressure regulator
5 Automatic supply
   valve
6 Burners
7 Combustion
   chamber
8 Heat exchanger
9 Chimney vent

Typical gas burner (equipped for circulating hot water)

Standard furnaces extract heat from the burners by means of a heat exchanger—a series of cells through which household air moves as it's warmed by the hot exhaust gases surrounding the outside of the cell walls. Such furnaces capture about 65 percent of generated heat . The rest goes up the chimney.

Condensing furnaces

To capture more of the wasted heat, condensing furnaces have a second heat exchanger that increases efficiency up to about 94 percent. However, because so much heat has been removed from the exhaust, it no longer rises through the chimney on its own. Therefore, these modern furnaces have induced-draft blowers to move the cool gases outdoors through plastic pipes. At these low temperatures, corrosive elements condense from the exhaust and must be drained away. Secondary heat exchangers must be highly corrosion resistant to handle the condensate that occurs.

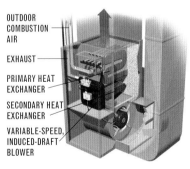

OUTDOOR COMBUSTION AIR

EXHAUST

PRIMARY HEAT EXCHANGER

SECONDARY HEAT EXCHANGER

VARIABLE-SPEED, INDUCED-DRAFT BLOWER

Combination boilers

Combination broilers provide both hot water for the heating system and a separte supply of instant hot water for taps and showers. Because there's no separate water heater the system is easier to install, takes up less space, and is more economical to operate.

Electric central heating systems have long been popular in Europe, and have been available in the United States for many years. Their popularity reached its peak during the 1960s, prior to the worldwide increase in energy costs, which has subsequently caused large-scale electric heating systems to be expensive to operate. Still, electric heat offers distinct advantages. It provides quick, efficient, draft-free warmth—and since no fuel is actually burned, there's no need for a chimney or fuel tank.

Because most electric systems operate on the principle of radiant, rather than convective, heat, they provide the most uniform heat and achieve their greatest energy efficiency when installed over the greatest possible area. Many small, low-intensity units covering a broad area produce better results than only a few high-intensity units widely spaced.

Baseboard heaters

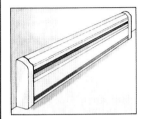

Electric baseboard heaters are the most popular form of electric heat in the United States. Each unit contains one or more horizontal heating elements, the entire unit being thermostatically controlled. Baseboard heaters are generally installed in groups that are controlled by a common thermostat. This makes it easy to independently adjust the heat in the various areas of the home.

Wall heaters

Individual electric wall heaters are often installed in special-use areas such as bathrooms and laundry rooms to provide supplementary or occasional heat. Installed between the studs of wall framing, most of these units include a small fan which aids in quickly circulating heated air throughout the room. Like baseboard heaters, these small wall heaters are thermostatically controlled.

Electric furnace

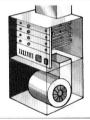

Like oil- or gas-fired forced-air furnaces, electric furnaces heat air which is then delivered throughout the house via ductwork. Electric furnaces, though, are small and require no fuel tank, chimney, or vents. They usually consist of several cookstove-type heating elements plus a squirrel-cage blower. While generally expensive to operate, electric furnaces can make sense where electricity is inexpensive and easy maintenance desired.

Radiant ceiling panels

Flexible and rigid panels containing electric heating grids are available for retrofitting or new construction. Some types fasten to standard framing prior to installation of the finished ceiling; others are embedded in gypsum and may be installed using drywall screws or nails.

Radiators and convectors

Steam units

The hot water from a boiler is pumped through the house along narrow pipes that are connected either to radiators or to special convector heaters. These units extract heat from the water and transfer it out to the objects and air in the room.

You can feel radiant heat being emitted directly from the hot surface of an appliance, but convected heat warms the air that comes into contact with the hot surface. As the warmed air rises toward the ceiling, it allows cooler air to flow in around the appliance, and this air in turn is warmed and moves upward. Eventually, a steady but very gentle circulation of air takes place in the room, and the temperature gradually rises until it reaches the setting on the room thermostat.

Radiators

Heat emission
As it's heated by the radiator, convected air flows upward and is replaced by cooler air near the base of the radiator. In addition, heat radiates from the surface of the panel.

Ordinary radiators are made of heavy cast iron which absorbs heat and then radiates it for a long time. For hot-water use only, lightweight radiators made of pressed sheetmetal are sometimes available as imports. In either type, water flows in through a manually adjustable valve at one corner and then out through a return valve at the other (except in the case of most steam radiators—see sidebar at right). A bleed valve is placed near the top of the radiator on the end opposite the inflow valve to let air out and prevent air locks, which stop the radiator from heating up properly. Cast-iron radiators are normally freestanding. However, special brackets are available to hang them from sturdy wall studs.

Sheetmetal radiators are usually hung on the wall.

Despite their name, radiators deliver only about half their output as radiant heat—the rest is emitted through natural convection as the surrounding air comes into contact with the hot surfaces of the radiator.

Radiators come in a wide range of sizes, and the larger they are, the greater their heat output. Maximum efficiency dictates that radiators be fully exposed in a room, not recessed or covered by a vented housing. Nor should they be painted or hidden behind furniture or drapes. A better way to deal with unsightly radiators is to replace them with less obtrusive convectors.

Cast-iron radiators designed for steam heat look similar to those used for hot water and, with minor modifications, are interchangeable. In most cases, steam radiators have only one pipe connecting them with the main supply line. Water that has condensed as the steam gives up its heat makes its way back to the boiler the way it came. In place of a bleed valve, steam radiators have an automatic vent built into the end of the radiator opposite the inlet pipe. The vent permits air to bleed out automatically as the radiator fills with steam. However, the steam itself does not escape.

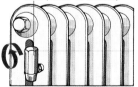

Curing knocking and banging
Many steam radiators produce knocking and banging noises as they heat up. The sound is actually made by water that has become trapped striking the walls of the radiator or piping as the steam seeks to get past. To cure the condition, make sure that the radiator slopes slightly downward toward the inlet pipe and the pipe itself slopes downward toward the boiler.

Uneven heating
If the radiator will not heat properly all the way across, suspect a blocked vent. Air that cannot escape prevents steam from diffusing throughout the radiator. Shortly after turning on the heat, unscrew the vent and remove it. As the steam rises, air should escape from the hole, followed by steam, indicating that the radiator itself is functioning properly. Buy a new vent and install it in place of the old one.

Cast-iron radiator
1 The manual valve controls incoming water.
2 The return valve controls water leaving the radiator, and is adjusted to keep the radiator hot.
3 The bleed valve purges the radiator of air.

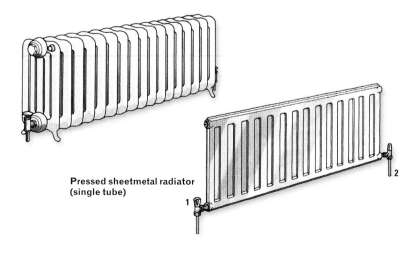

Pressed sheetmetal radiator (single tube)

Most modern hot-water systems use relatively inexpensive convection heaters. Unlike radiators, convection heaters emit none of their heat in the form of direct radiation. The water from the boiler passes through a finned pipe inside the heater. The fins absorb the heat and transfer it to the air around them. Once the air warms, it moves up and escapes through an opening at the top of the heater. At the same time, cool air is drawn in through the open bottom to replace the air that left.

Most convection heaters have a damper that can be set to control the airflow; many are designed to be mounted at baseboard level, similar to electric heating units. A variation on the basic convection heater is one with a fan that accelerates airflow across the heated fins, resulting in faster heating.

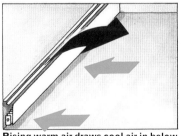
Rising warm air draws cool air in below

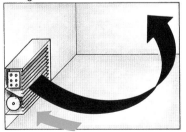
Airflow by fan-assisted convection

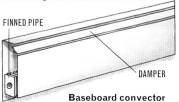
FINNED PIPE

DAMPER

Baseboard convector

A t one time, central heating radiators or convectors were nearly always placed under windows to offset the cold glass surfaces and cut the drafts caused by warmed air cooling against them. However, with modern, thermally-effective double-glazed windows these problems are less severe and you can place radiators or convectors with an eye to maximum comfort.

Convenience and cost

Your radiators and convection heaters can be positioned anywhere that's convenient. However, it's best to keep in mind the shape of the room and the distance from the boiler, so costly pipe runs are kept to a reasonable minimum.

While double glazing means that the heaters don't necessarily need to be placed under the windows, there is a slight drawback to placing them against walls. The warm air rising from them will tend to discolor the paint or wallpaper above. You can guard against this by fitting radiator shelves immediately above them to direct the warm air away from the walls.

Never hang curtains or stand furniture in front of radiators or convectors. They will absorb radiated heat, and curtains will trap convected heat between themselves and the walls. While convectors radiate almost no heat, you should never prevent warm air from leaving the heater nor cool air from being drawn into it.

A room's shape should also affect your decisions regarding the positioning of heaters and how many you need. For example, you cannot heat a large L-shaped room from a single radiator in its short end. A heating contractor can determine the number and sizes of units required and the best placement of each.

Selecting the size of heaters

A house loses heat whenever a door or window is opened and by conduction through the actual materials that make up its doors, windows, walls, floors, ceilings, and roof. To work out the heating needs of the rooms in a house, the heating contractor has to take into account the rate at which they lose heat. This varies with the materials and construction. The temperature on the other side of walls, floors, and ceilings comes into the equation.

The contractor also needs to know the temperature to which each room must be heated, and there are standard levels for particular rooms. A heat-loss analysis will be made to produce the heating requirement for each room, and radiators or convectors are selected with the appropriate outputs. Then all the heat output figures are totaled to give the output required from the boiler.

When you install your central heating, be sure to choose radiators and convection heaters that meet the standards approved by your local building inspector.

Ideal room temperatures
While most of us are happy to choose our room temperatures to suit our lifestyles and tastes, the professional who designs your heating system will make certain assumptions and may offer you suggestions. The following chart is an example of temperature settings for particular areas in the home. It may be used as a starting point for designing the system that suits you best.

ROOM TEMPERATURE	
Living room	70°F (21°C)
Dining room	70°F (21°C)
Kitchen	60°F (16°C)
Hall/landing	65°F (18°C)
Bedroom	60°F (16°C)
Bathroom	72°F (23°C)

Heating system controls

Zone control valves

Room thermostat

Programmer or timer

A range of automatic control systems and devices for circulating central heating can, if used sensibly, enable you to make real savings in operating costs There are three main types: temperature controllers (thermostats), automatic on/off switches (timers and programmers), and heating circuit controllers (zone valves).

Thermostats

All steam and hot-water systems incorporate thermostats to prevent overheating. A gas- or oil-fired tank will have one that can be set to alter heat output by switching the unit on and off. Another, called an aquastat, can be set to monitor the temperature of the water circulating through the pipes.

Room thermostats are common forms of central heating control, often the only ones fitted. They are placed in rooms where temperatures usually remain fairly stable, and work on the assumption that any rise or drop in room temperature will be matched by similar ones throughout the house. Room thermostats control temperatures through simple on/off switching of the heating unit, or its pump if a boiler must run constantly to provide a constant supply of domestic hot water.

The room thermostat's drawback is that it can make no allowance for local temperature changes in other rooms caused, for example, by the sun shining through a window or a separate heater being switched on. Much more sophisticated temperature control is provided by thermostatic radiator valves, which can be fitted to radiators instead of the standard manually operated inlet valves. Temperature sensors open and close them, varying heat output to maintain the desired temperatures in individual rooms.

Thermostatic radiator valves need not be fitted in every room. You can use one to reduce the heat in a kitchen or reduce the temperature in a bathroom while using a room thermostat to regulate the temperature in the rest of the house or in separate zones.

Other available thermostatic controls include devices for regulating the temperature of domestic hot water and for giving frost protection to a unit switched off during winter vacations.

It is not often that all the rooms in a house are in use at once. During the day it is normal for the upstairs rooms to be unused for long periods, and to heat them continuously would be wasteful. A better idea is to divide your system into heating zones—the usual ones being upstairs and downstairs—and heat those areas only when it's necessary.

Control is provided by motorized valves linked to a timer that directs the flow of hot water through preselected pipes at specific times. Alternatively, zone valves can be used to provide zone temperature control by being linked to individual zone thermostats. In many cases, circulator pumps piped to specific zones and controlled by thermostats do the same job.

A motorized zone-control valve

Timers and programmers

A timer can be set to switch a heating system on and off to suit your family's schedule. It can switch on and warm the house before you get up, then off again before you go to work, on again when you come home, and so on.

The simpler timers offer two "on" and two "off" settings which are repeated daily, though a manual override allows variations for weekends and such. More sophisticated programmers offer a number of on/off options.

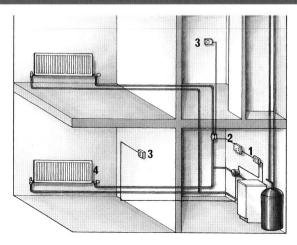

Heating controls
1 Programmable type controls the boiler and pump.
2 A timer is used to control a zone valve. It can be used to regulate boiler and pump.
3 Room thermometer controls pump or a zone valve.
4 A nonelectric radiator valve controls an individual heater.

Furnace maintenance

Whether you have a gas or an oil furnace, you can arrange a regular maintenance contract with the original installer or the fuel supplier

Gas-fired installations

Many gas utilities offer a choice of service arrangements for gas furnaces. These cover their own installations, but they can often be arranged for systems put in by other installers on the condition that the utility inspects the installation before writing the contract.

The simplest maintenance plan provides for an annual check and adjustment of the furnace. If any repairs are needed, either at the time of the regular check or at other times during the year, the labor and the required parts will be charged separately. But, for an extra fee it is possible to have both free labor and free parts for furnace repairs at any time of the year. Most utilities will also extend the arrangement to include a check of the whole heating system at the same time that the furnace is checked.

Your own installer may be able to offer you a similar choice of service plans. The best course is to compare charges and decide which gives the best value for your money.

Oil-fired installations

The installers of oil-fired systems and the suppliers of fuel oil offer service plans similar to those outlined above. These range from a simple annual checkup to complete coverage for new parts and labor if and when repairs become necessary.

Routine cleaning, maintenance, and adjustment will give your central heating furnace a longer life and prolong its efficiency.

Both gas- and oil-fired furnaces should be serviced once a year by qualified service persons, but you can do a certain amount of cleaning and tuning up yourself.

Maintaining gas burners

Because gas furnaces involve less complicated equipment and technology than oil burners (combining gas and air for combustion is much easier than combining fuel oil and air), frequent maintenance of gas furnaces is less necessary than with oil-fired units. Inspection of the flame and pilot mechanisms should be carried out yearly by a professional service technician, of course. Cleaning—a task suitable for do-it-yourselfers—normally need take place only every two or three years. Before beginning any maintenance task, be certain to turn off the main gas supply line, pilot light, and burners.

Servicing oil burners

Here are several maintenance chores you can perform that do not involve adjusting the combustion components of the furnace. Unless you are skilled and have the proper testing instruments, leave that to a service professional. Before starting any maintenance task, turn the furnace completely off.

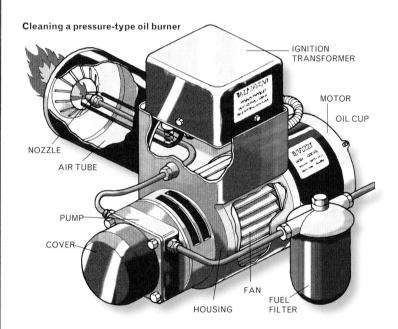

Cleaning a pressure-type oil burner

IGNITION TRANSFORMER
MOTOR
OIL CUP
NOZZLE
AIR TUBE
PUMP
COVER
FAN
HOUSING
FUEL FILTER

Change fuel filter
Place pan beneath filter area. Unscrew cup. Remove and replace cartridge and gasket.

Lubricate motor
Locate oil cups at each end of motor (if none are present, motor is maintenance free). Squirt 3 to 6 drops of 10W nondetergent electric motor oil in each cup. Do not over-lubricate.

Clean fan
Unbolt transformer and swing aside to access fan. Clean blades with bottle brush or lint-free cloth attached to stick; wipe interior of housing with rag.

Clean pump strainer
Remove pump cover and gasket. Soak strainer in solvent, then brush clean with toothbrush. Replace using new gasket. (Note: Some pumps do not have strainers.)

Draining a hot-water system

Circulating hot-water systems rarely need complete draining. However, if the water has become overly contaminated, or if a component fails and must be replaced, the task of removing the water from the boiler and piping can be done fairly easily.

Draining the system

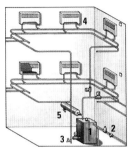

The most frequent reason for draining a hot-water system is excessive rust in the circulating water. Each year, a small amount of water should be drained from the boiler into a clear glass by way of the draincock (usually located near the unit's base). If the water appears unusually cloudy, drain the system, then flush it clean and refill it.

Begin by turning off the furnace. Remember that with a gas furnace this means also turning off the pilot flame and main gas inlet. Next, turn off the water supply line to the boiler. Connect a garden hose to the draincock and lead the other end of the hose to a floor drain. If no drain is present, position a bucket beneath the draincock. After waiting until you are certain the water has cooled sufficiently, open the draincock and let the water drain out. While it is draining, open the bleed valves on the radiators in the house to avoid creating a partial vacuum (which prevents complete drainage). At the same time, drain the expansion tank (see below).

To rid the boiler of accumulated rust and sediment, flush it by leaving the draincock open after the water stops flowing, then reopen the water supply line to admit fresh water into the system. When the water runs clear, close the draincock and let the boiler fill.

To refill the boiler, close the draincock used for flushing the system. To add a commercial rust inhibitor, close the water supply line, remove the pressure-relief valve from the boiler tank and pour the recommended amount of inhibitor into the hole. Replace the valve and reopen the water supply line. Wait until the boiler fills, then turn on the furnace. Close the radiator bleed valves when you hear water rising in the radiators. Wait several hours with the system running, then bleed all the radiators.

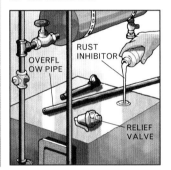

Draining the expansion tank

Conventional expansion tanks are merely cylinders partially filled with water. As the water in the circulating system heats and expands, air present in the tank is compressed, relieving the excess system pressure and also keeping the hot water from turning to steam. Over time, most tanks gradually accumulate too much water, which forces the air out and prevents the tank from working properly. The solution is to drain the tank, an operation that must also be done if the entire system is to be drained.

To drain a conventional tank, attach a garden hose to the draincock (it's usually under the tank). Close off the inlet pipe leading to the tank, then open the draincock. If no inlet valve is present, you must drain the entire system in order to drain the tank.

Diaphragm expansion tanks
Some expansion tanks physically separate air and water by means of a rubber partition, or diaphragm, that divides the tank into two chambers. Instead of draining the water from such tanks, periodically recharge them with air. To do the job, first check the air pressure in the chamber using an ordinary tire-pressure gauge attached to the recharge valve, usually located on the underside of the tank. Then use a bicycle pump or compressor to add air until the gauge indicates that you've reached the tank's recommended pressure. If you find that your diaphragm tank requires even moderately frequent recharging, there's a good chance that it's leaking and should be replaced.

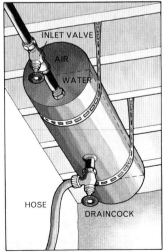

Conventional expansion tank

You can remove an individual radiator while the wall behind it is decorated without having to drain the whole system. You simply close the valves at the ends of the radiator, drain it, and then remove it.

Shut off both valves, turning the shank of the return valve clockwise with a key or an adjustable wrench (1). Note the number of turns need-ed to close it so you can reopen it by the same number of turns later.

Make sure that you have plenty of rags for mopping up spills, a jug, and a large bowl, as the water in the radiator will be very dirty. Also, roll back the floorcovering before you start, if possible.

Unscrew the capnut that holds one of the valves to the adapter in the end of the radiator (2). Hold the jug under the joint and open the bleed valve slowly to let the water drain out. Transfer the water from jug to bowl and keep going until no more can be drained.

Unscrew the capnut that holds the other valve on the radiator. If the radiator is not freestanding, lift it free from its wall brackets (3) and drain any remaining water into the bowl. Unscrew the wall brackets to decorate.

To replace the radiator after decorating, screw the brackets back in place, hang the radiator on them, and tighten the capnuts on both valves. Close the bleed valve and open both radiator valves. Adjust the return valve by the same number of turns you used to close it. Finally, use the bleed valve to release any trapped air.

Trapped air prevents radiators from fully heating through, and regular intake of air can cause corrosion. If a radiator feels cooler at the top than at the bottom, it's likely that a pocket of air has formed inside it and stopped circulation of the water. Getting the air out of a radiator, or bleeding it, is a simple procedure.

Opening a bleed valve

Bleed radiators with the circulator running. Each radiator has a bleed valve at one of its top corners, near the end opposite the water inlet. Usually the valve is slotted for a screwdriver, but on many new models the valve has a square-section shank in the center of the round plug. The installer should have given you a key to fit the shanks, but if not, you can buy one at a plumbing supply store.

Use the key to turn the valve shank counterclockwise a quarter of a turn. It shouldn't be necessary to turn it farther, but have a small jar handy to catch spurting water if you open the valve too far. You will hear a hissing sound as the air escapes. Keep the key on the shank of the valve, and when the hissing stops and the first dribble of water appears, close the valve tightly.

Under no circumstances should you open the valve any more than is needed to let the air out, or remove it completely, as this will produce a deluge of water.

Releasing trapped air in a radiator.
If your radiator requires a key, keep it in a handy place, where you can find it on short notice.

Fitting an automatic bleed valve

If you find yourself having to bleed one particular radiator regularly, it will save you trouble if you replace its bleed valve with an automatic one that will allow air to escape but not water.

To do the job, first drain the water from the system, then use your bleed-valve key to unscrew the old valve completely out of the drain plug (1). Wind some Teflon tape around the threads of the auto-matic valve (2) and screw it finger-tight into the blanking plug (3).

Refill the system; if any water appears around the threads of the new valve, tighten it farther with an adjustable wrench (4).

If, when the system is going again, the radiator still feels cool on top, it may be that a larger amount of air has collected than the new bleed valve can cope with. In this case, unscrew the valve until you hear air hissing out. Tighten it again when the hissing stops and the first trickle of water appears.

1 Unscrew old valve

2 Tape new threads

3 Screw it fingertight

4 Stop any leak in use

1 Close valve

2 Unscrew capnut

3 Final draining
Lift radiator from brackets and drain off any remaining water.

Radiator valves

Like faucets, radiator valves can develop leaks—which are usually relatively easy to cure. Occasionally, however, it's necessary to replace a faulty valve.

VALVE HEAD

GLAND NUT

Tightening gland nut
Tighten the gland nut with a wrench to stop a leak from a radiator valve spindle. If the leak persists, replace the valve.

Curing a leaking radiator valve

If an inlet valve or return valve on a radiator seems to be leaking, it's most likely that one of the capnuts that secures it to the water pipe and to the radiator's valve adapter needs some tightening up.

Tighten the suspect capnut with an adjustable wrench while you hold the body of the valve with a pipe wrench to prevent it from moving. If this doesn't work, the valve will have to be replaced.

If the leak seems to be from the valve adapter in the radiator, the joint will have to be repaired in the same way as when a new valve is fitted (see below). If the leak seems to be from the valve spindle, tighten the gland nut (see left) or replace the valve.

If the ferrule is jammed onto the pipe, cut the pipe off below floorboard level and make up a new section. Join it to the old pipe by means of either a soldered joint or a compression joint.

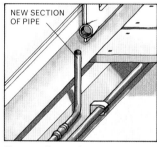

NEW SECTION OF PIPE

New section replaces pipe with jammed ferrule

Replacing a worn or damaged valve

Be sure that the new valve is exactly like the old one, or it may not align with the water pipe. Drain the heating system and lay rags under the valve to catch any remaining water that may come out.

Hold the body of the valve with a pipe wrench and use an adjustable wrench to unscrew the capnuts that hold the valve to the water pipe and to the adapter in the end of the radiator **(1)**. Lift the valve from the end of the pipe **(2)**. If the valve being replaced is a return valve, don't remove it before you have closed it, counting the number of turns needed so that you can open the new valve by the same number to balance the radiator. Unscrew the adapter from the radiator **(3)**. You may be able to do this with an adjustable wrench, or you may need an Allen wrench, depending on the adapter.

Fitting the new valve
Ensure that the threads in the end of the radiator are clean and wind Teflon tape four or five times around the thread of the new valve's adapter, then screw it into the end of the radiator by hand and tighten it further one and one-half turns with

an adjustable or Allen wrench.

Slide the valve capnut and a new ferrule over the end of the water pipe and fit the valve to the end of the pipe **(4)**, but don't tighten the capnuts yet. First align the valve body with the adapter and tighten the capnut that holds them together **(5)**. Hold the valve body firm with a wrench while you do this. Now tighten the capnut that holds the valve to the water pipe **(6)**.

Finally, refill the system, check for leaks, and tighten the capnuts again if necessary.

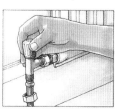

1 Hold valve firm and loosen both capnuts

2 Unscrew capnuts and lift valve out

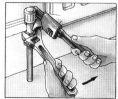

3 Remove valve adapter from radiator

4 Fit new adapter, then fit new valve on pipe

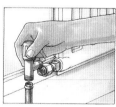

5 Connect valve to adapter and tighten capnut

6 Tighten capnut that holds valve to pipe

Replacing a radiator

Try to obtain a new radiator exactly the same size as the one you're planning to replace. This makes the job relatively easy.

Simple replacement

Drain and remove the old radiator. Once it's away from the wall, unscrew the valve adapters from the bottom with an adjustable wrench or, if necessary, an Allen wrench. Unscrew the bleed valve with its key, and then the two drain plugs from the top of the radiator, using a square or hexagonal Allen wrench **(1)**.

With steel wool, clean up the threads of both adapters and both plugs **(2)**, then wind four or five turns of Teflon tape around the threads **(3)**. Screw them into the new radiator and install the bleed valve into the plug.

Position the new radiator and connect the valves to their adapters. Open the valves and fill and bleed the radiators.

1 Removing the plug
Use an Allen wrench to unscrew the drain plug at the end of the radiator.

2 Cleaning the threads
Use steel wool to clean any corrosion from the threads of both drain plugs and valve adapters.

3 Taping the threads
Make the threaded joints watertight by wrapping Teflon tape several times around each component before screwing them into the new radiator.

Installing a different radiator

The replacement job will require somewhat more work if you can't get a radiator of the same type as the old one. If the replacement is not freestanding, you'll have to fit new wall brackets. Possibly, you'll also have to alter the water pipes.

Drain the system. Then, for a wall-hung unit, take the old brackets off the wall. Lay the new radiator facedown on the floor and slide one of its brackets onto the hangers welded to the back of the radiator. Measure from the top of the bracket to the bottom of the radiator, add 4 or 5 inches for clearance under the radiator, then mark a horizontal line on the wall that distance from the floor. Now measure the distance between the centers of the radiator hangers and make two marks on the horizontal line that distance apart and at equal distances from the two water pipes **(1)**.

Line up the brackets with the pencil marks, mark their mounting screw holes, drill and plug the holes, and install the brackets **(2)**.

Lift up the floorboards below the radiator and cut off the vertical portions of the inlet and return pipes. Connect the valves to the radiator and hang it on its brackets. Slip a short length of pipe into each valve as a guide for any further trimming of the pipes. Solder these lengths to the original pipes **(3)**, then connect the new pipes to the valves. Refill the system and check for leaks.

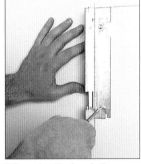

2 Securing the brackets
Screw the mounting brackets to the wall.

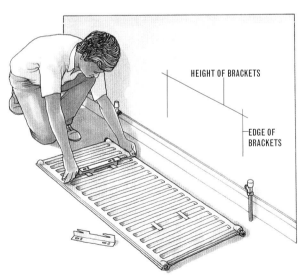

HEIGHT OF BRACKETS

EDGE OF BRACKETS

1 Transferring the measurements
Measure the positions of the radiator brackets and transfer these dimensions to the wall.

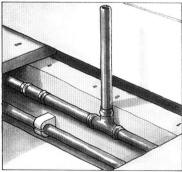

3 Connecting the new pipework
Make sure the vertical section of pipe aligns with the radiator valve.

Servicing circulator pumps

Open bleed valve with screwdriver

Forced hot-water heating depends on a steady cycle of hot water, from boiler to radiators and back to the boiler, for reheating. This is the pump's job. A faulty pump means poor circulation. A failed pump means no circulation.

Bleeding the pump

If your radiators don't seem to be warming up, though you can hear or feel the pump running, it's likely that an air lock has formed in the pump and its impeller is spinning in air. The air must be bled from the pump, a job that's done in the same way as bleeding a radiator. You'll find a screw-in valve for the purpose in the pump's outer casing. The

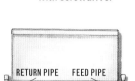

1 Clip thermometers to radiator pipes

valve's position varies with different makes, but it is usually marked.

Switch off the pump, have a jar on hand to catch any water, and open the valve with a screwdriver or vent key. Open it just until you hear air hissing out. When the hissing stops and water appears, close the valve fully.

Adjusting the pump

There are two kinds of circulator pumps: fixed-head and variable-head. Fixed-head units run at a single speed, forcing the water to move through the system at a fixed rate. Variable-head pumps can be adjusted to run at different speeds, circulating the water at different rates.

When a variable-head pump is fitted as part of a hot-water system, the installer adjusts its speed after balancing all the radiators so that each room reaches its optimum temperature. If you find that your rooms are not as warm as you would like, though you have opened the radiator valves fully, you can adjust the pump speed. But first check that all radiators show the same temperature drop between their inlets and outlets. You can get clip-on thermometers for the job from a plumber's

2 Adjust pump speed to alter temperature

Bridging the gap
Modern pumps are sometimes smaller than equivalent older models. If this is the case, buy a converter designed to bridge the gap between the existing pipes.

supply store. You will need a pair of them.

Clip one thermometer to the feed pipe just below the radiator valve and the other to the return pipe below its valve **(1)**. The difference between the temperatures registered by the two should be about 20°F. If it is not, uncover the return valve and close it further (to increase the difference) or open it more (to reduce the difference).

Having balanced the radiators, you can now adjust the pump. Switch it off and then turn the speed adjustment up **(2)**, one step at a time, until you are getting the overall temperatures you want. You may be able to work the adjustment by hand, or you may need some special tool, such as an Allen wrench, depending on the make and model of your pump.

Replacing a worn pump

If you have to replace your circulator pump, be quite sure that the one you buy is of exactly the same make and model as the old one. If that's not possible, get advice from a service technician.

Turn off the boiler and close the isolating valves on each side of the pump. If there are no isolating valves, you will have to drain the whole system.

Find the electrical circuit that supplies the circulating pump and shut off the circuit breaker at the service panel. Then, take the coverplate off the pump and disconnect its wiring **(1)**.

Have a bowl or bucket on hand to catch any water left in the pump, and use old rags for any mopping up that you may have to do. Undo the retaining nuts that hold the pump to the valves or the pipes with an adjustable wrench **(2)** and catch the water as it flows out.

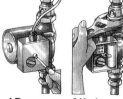

1 Remove coverplate | **2 Undo connecting nuts**

3 Attach new pump | **4 Connect wires**

Remove the pump and fit the new one in its place, taking care to properly install any sealing washers that are provided with the new unit **(3)**. Then tighten the retaining nuts.

Take the coverplate off the new pump, feed in the electrical cable, connect the wires to the pump's terminals **(4)**, and replace the coverplate. If the pump is of the variable-head type (see above), set the speed control to the speed indicated on the old pump.

Open both isolating valves (or if the system has been drained, refill it). Check the pump connections for leaks and tighten them if necessary. Then open the pump's bleed valve to release any air that may have become trapped in it. Finally, switch the pump's circuit breaker on at the service panel and test the pump.

Control valves

Control valves are a means by which timers and thermostats adjust heating levels. Worn or faulty valves can seriously impair the reliability of the system, and should therefore be repaired or replaced promptly.

Replacing a faulty valve

Make sure the new valve is exactly the same as the one you are replacing.

Drain the system. Turn off power to the valve by removing the fuse or switching off the circuit breaker that protects the heating system's circuit.

The cable from the valve will be wired to an adjacent junction box, which is also connected to the heating system's other controls. Remove the cover and disconnect the valve wiring. Make a note of the terminals used, so it will be easy to connect the new unit.

To remove the old valve, cut through the pipe on each side **(1)**. When installing the new valve, bridge the gap with short sections of pipe and slip couplings **(2)**. After soldering the slip couplings, tighten the valve capnuts **(3)**. Connect the valve's cable to the junction box, then turn on the power to the circuit.

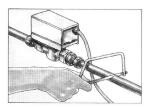

1 Removing the valve
If you're unable to disconnect the valve, use a hacksaw to cut through the pipe on each side.

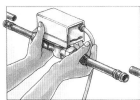
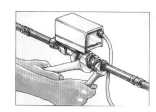

2 Fitting the new valve
With the new valve connected to short pipes, slide the slip couplings along the stubs and fit the assembly to the existing piping.

3 Tightening the nuts
After soldering the joints, tighten the valve capnuts on each side, using two open-end wrenches. Refill heating system and check that the valve is working properly.

Two-port control valve
A two-port valve seals off a section of pipe when the water has reached the required temperature.

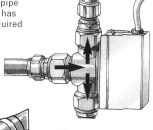

Three-port control valve
This type of valve can isolate the central heating from the hot-water circuit.

Slip couplings
A slip coupling slides along the pipe, so it's easy to bridge gaps in fixed lengths of piping.

Replacing a valve motor

If a motorized valve won't open, its electric motor may have failed. Before replacing the motor, use a voltage tester to see whether it's receiving power. If it is, install a new motor.

There is no need to drain the system. Switch off the electrical supply to the heating system at the service panel—don't merely turn off the programmer, as motorized valves have a permanent live feed.

Once the power is off, remove the cover and undo the single screw that holds the motor in place **(1)**. Open the valve, using the manual lever, and lift out the motor **(2)**. Disconnect the two motor wires by cutting off the connectors.

Insert a new motor—available from a plumbing supply dealer—and let the lever spring back to the closed position. Install and tighten the retaining screw. Strip the ends and connect the wires, using the new connectors **(3)**.

Replace the valve cover and test the operation by turning on the power and running the system.

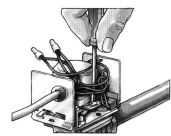

1 Releasing the motor retaining screw
Remove cover and then retaining screw

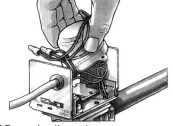

2 Removing the motor
Push lever to open valve, then lift out motor

3 Fitting the new motor
Join wires, using two supplied connectors

Hot-water radiant heat

With the availability of reliable plastic tubing, sophisticated controls, and efficient insulation, in-floor, hot-water radiant heat has become a viable and affordable form of central heating. Manufacturers have developed a range of systems to suit virtually any situation. The same companies generally offer a design service aimed at providing a heating system that satisfies the customer's specific requirements. In many cases, the technology can be applied to older homes, as well as to new construction.

An in-floor heating system radiates heat more evenly and over a wider area than a standard hot-water system. This reduces hot and cold spots within the room and produces a more comfortable environment.

Radiant heating is also energy-efficient, because it operates at a lower temperature than other central heating systems. And because temperature is more even throughout a room, the thermostat can be set a degree or two lower, yet the house still feels warm and cozy.

● **Maintaining in-floor heating**
The heating elements are virtually maintenance-free. If the flow through the pipework becomes restricted, the circuit can be flushed with water by attaching a hose to the manifold.

Underfloor heating systems

In-floor heating can be incorporated in any type of floor construction, including solid concrete floors and various types of wood flooring. The heat emanates from a continuous length of plastic tubing that snakes across the floor, forming parallel loops and covering an area of one or more rooms.

The entire system is divided into separate zones to provide custom temperature control in specific areas. Each zone is controlled by a thermostat, and is connected to a multivalve manifold that forms the heart of

the system. The manifold controls the temperature of the water and the flow rate to the various zones. Once a room or zone reaches its required temperature, a valve automatically shuts off that part of the circuit. A flow meter for each of the zones allows the circuits to be balanced when setting up the system, and subsequently monitors system performance.

The manifold, which is installed in an accessible place above floor level, is connected to the boiler through a conventional circulation pump.

Getting started
To do the work yourself, first locate a supplier who can provide instructions and a plan for your project. The company will need a detailed description of your planned extension and a drawing of your house, including specs of your present hot-water system. You'll then receive a schematic of the new system and the price for all the components.

The simplest type of system is connected to the pipework of the existing radiator circuit. Heat for the extension will be available only when the existing hot-water system is running, although temperature in the extension can be controlled independently by a thermostat connected to a motorized zone valve and the in-floor hot-water heating pump. For full control, the flow and return pipes for the in-floor system must be connected directly to the boiler, and the thermostat wired to switch the boiler on and off and to control the temperature in the new space.

If it's impossible to utilize the existing heating system, or if the boiler has insufficient capacity, you'll need to install a separate boiler and pump system to heat the extension.

Installation methods

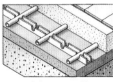

1 Concrete floor

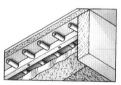

2 Floating-wood floor

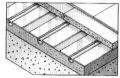

3 Standard wooden floor

When radiant heating is installed in a new building, the plastic tubes are often set into a solid concrete floor **(1)**. Flooring insulation is laid over the base concrete, and rows of special pipe clips are fixed to the insulation. (Sometimes a metal mesh is used instead of the clips.) The flexible heating tubes are then clipped into place at the required spacings, and a concrete slab is poured on top.

With a floating-wood floor **(2)**, a layer of grooved insulation is laid over the concrete base, and the pipes are set in aluminum diffusion plates inserted in the grooves. The entire floor area is

then covered with an edge-bonded chipboard or a similar underlayment.

The heating pipes can be fastened with spacer clips to the underside of a standard wooden floor **(3)**. In this situation, clearance holes are drilled through the joists at strategic points to permit a continuous run of pipework. Reflective foil and thick blanket insulation are then installed below the pipes.

It is possible to lay the pipes on top of an existing floor, but this method raises the floor level by the thickness of the pipe assembly and the new flooring.

Added to an existing radiator system, in-floor hot-water heating makes a good choice for heating a new extension. The concrete slab that might be used for such a project provides an ideal base for this form of heating.

The basic plumbing system

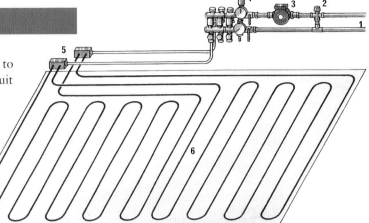

Your supplier will suggest the best point to connect the new plumbing to the existing hot-water circuit. It can be at any convenient point, provided that radiator performance is not be affected.

The pipes connecting the manifold for the in-floor heating to the radiator circuit can be metal or plastic, and they can be the same size as (but not larger than) the existing pipes. Again, your supplier will advise what to use.

The flow and return pipes from the manifold to the house extension circuit (illustrated here, as an example) are connected to individual zone distributors, which in turn are connected to the flexible underfloor-heating tubes.

Basic system
1 Flow and return pipes from existing central heating circuit
2 Water-temperature mixing valve
3 Pump
4 Manifold with zone valves
5 Zone distributors
6 Radiant-heating tube

Constructing the floor

To build an extension that will be served by radiant hot-water heat, you will need to excavate the site and pour a concrete slab that conforms to your local building codes. Check with your codes office for details. The slab should include a vapor barrier. Allow for a layer of floor insulation under the slab—a minimum of 2-inch, flooring-grade expanded polystyrene or 1¼-inch extruded polyurethane (check with

your building inspector). The floor should be finished with a 2½-inch concrete slab, plus the preferred floor covering.

When laying the floor insulation slabs, install a strip of 1-inch-thick insulation around the edges. This is to prevent cold from penetrating the baseboard and the floor slab.

Cut a hole through the house wall to connect the new system to the old.

Floor construction
1 Gravel
2 Vapor barrier
3 Concrete base
4 Insulation
5 Edge insulation
6 Pipe clips and pipe
7 Floor slab
8 Floor tiles

Installing the system

Mount the manifold in a convenient place and connect the two distributor blocks below it—one for the flow, the other for the return. Run the flow and return pipes back into the house, ready for connecting to the existing central heating circuit. Install your new pump and a mixing valve in the flow and return pipes.

Following the system maker's layout, press the spikes of the pipe clips into the insulation at the prescribed spacing **(1)**. Lay out the heating tubes for both coils, and clip them into place. Push one end of one of the coils into the flow distributor, and the other end into the return distributor

(2). Connect the other coil similarly.

Connect flow and return pipes to the house's hot-water system—it pays to insert a pair of isolating valves now, so that you can shut off the new circuit for maintenance. Fill, flush out, and check the new system for leaks.

Pour concrete composed of 4 parts sand and 1 part cement, with a plasticizer additive. Let it set for at least three weeks before laying the floor covering—don't use heat to accelerate the drying.

Fit the thermostat at head height, out of direct sunlight. Make the electrical connections, then set the thermostat to control the circuit pump and zone valve, following supplied instructions.

1 Press pipe clips into place

2 Push tubing into distributors

Hissing or banging sounds from boiler or pipework

Overheating caused by:

- Blocked chimney (with coal furnace).
  Check flueway for substantial soot fall. Sweep chimney.

- Heavy mineral deposits in system due to hard water.
  Shut down boiler and pump. Treat system with a descaler, then drain, flush, and refill system.

- Faulty boiler thermostat.
  Shut down boiler. Leave pump working to circulate water, to cool system quickly. When it's cool, operate boiler thermostat control. If you don't hear a clicking sound, call in a repair person.

- Incorrectly sloping pipework (with steam systems).
  Check to see that radiators and pipe runs carrying steam slope downward at all points so that water can travel freely back to boiler. Insert wooden wedges under improperly sloping radiators. Rehang improperly pitched pipe. Check results using spirit level.

- Circulating pump not working (with coal furnace).
  Shut down boiler, then check that the pump is switched on. If pump won't work, turn off power and check wired connections to it. If pump seems to be running but outlet pipe is cool, check for air lock by using bleed screw. If pump is still not working, shut it down, drain system, remove pump, and check it for blockage. Clean pump or replace it if necessary.

Pressure-relief valve on circulating hot-water boiler opens, sending water through overflow pipe

- Excess pressure in piping caused by malfunctioning expansion tank.
  Drain conventional tank by first closing inlet valve leading to tank, then opening draincock on underside of tank. For tanks with diaphragm design, recharge air chamber using bicycle pump, or replace tank.

All radiators remain cool, though boiler is operating normally

- Pump not working.
  Check pump by listening or feeling for motor vibration. If pump is running, check for air lock by opening bleed valve. If this has no effect, the pump outlet may be blocked. Switch off boiler and pump, remove pump, and clean or replace as necessary.

- Pump thermostat or timer is set incorrectly or is faulty.
  Check thermostat or timer setting and reset if necessary. If this makes no difference, switch off power and check wiring connections. If connections are in good order, call in repair person.

Radiators in one part of house do not warm up

- Timer or thermostat that controls zone valve faulty or not set properly.
  Check timer or thermostat setting and reset if necessary. If this has no effect, switch off the power supply and check wired connections. If this makes no difference, call in repair person.

- Zone valve itself faulty.
  Drain system and replace valve.

Single radiator does not warm up

- Manual inlet valve closed.
  Check valve setting and open if needed.

- Thermostatic radiator valve faulty or not set properly.
  Check setting of valve and reset it if necessary. If this has no effect, drain radiator and replace valve.

- Return valve not set properly.
  Remove return-valve cover and adjust valve setting until radiator seems as warm as those in adjacent rooms. Have valve properly balanced during next service visit.

- Inlet/outlet blocked by corrosion.
  Close inlet and return valves, remove radiator; flush out and refit or replace as necessary.

Area at top of radiator stays cool while the bottom is warm

- Air lock at top of radiator preventing water from circulating fully.
  Operate bleed valve to release the trapped air.

Cool patch in center of radiator while top and ends are warm

- Heavy deposits of corrosion at bottom of radiator are restricting circulation of water.
  Close inlet and return valves, remove radiator, flush out, then refit or replace as necessary.

Water leaking from system

- Loose pipe unions at joints, pump connections, boiler connections, etc.
  Switch off boiler and turn furnace off completely; switch off pump and tighten leaking joints. If this has no effect, drain the system and remake joints completely.

- Split or punctured pipes.
  Wrap damaged pipes in rags temporarily, switch off boiler and pump, and make a temporary repair with hose or commercial leak sealant. Drain system and fit new pipe.

Boiler not working

- Thermostat set too low.
  Check that room or boiler thermostat is set correctly.

- Timer or programmer not working.
  Check that unit is switched on and set correctly. Have it replaced if the fault persists.

- Pilot light goes out.
  Relight a gas-boiler pilot light following the manufacturer's instructions, which are usually found on the back of the boiler's front panel. If the pilot fails to ignite after second try, have the unit replaced.

Plumber's tool kit

PLUMBER'S AND METALWORKER'S TOOLS

While easy-to-work plastic pipe is used extensively in residential plumbing, particularly for drain and vent systems, it only comprises part of the plumbing picture. Brass fittings and pipe made from copper dominate typical water supply systems, and cast-iron waste and vent pipe is still found in many older homes. Therefore, a good part of a plumber's tool kit includes tools for working with metal.

EQUIPMENT FOR REMOVING BLOCKAGES

You don't have to get a plumber to clear blocked fixtures, pipes, or even large drains. All the necessary equipment can be bought or rented.

Plunger

This is a simple but effective tool for clearing a blockage from a sink, toilet, or bath. A pumping action on the rubber cup forces air and water along the pipe to disperse the blockage. When you buy a plunger, make sure the cup is large enough to cover the drain. If you have more than one bathroom, buy one for each.

Drain auger

A flexible coiled-wire drain auger will pass through small-diameter waste pipes to clear blockages. Pass the corkscrew-like head into the waste pipe until it reaches the blockage, clamp the cranked handle onto the other end, and then turn it to rotate the head and engage the blockage. Push and pull the auger till the pipe is clear.

Also available are rotary drain augers that are powered by an electric drill. These may have a reach of 20 feet and are capable of navigating the tight turns in drain traps.

Small-wire auger

The short, coiled-wire drainpipe auger is designed for clearing toilets and drain traps. To operate it, the handle is rotated in a rigid, hollow shaft while the auger end is pushed into the drain. The auger has a vinyl guard to keep the fixture from getting scratched.

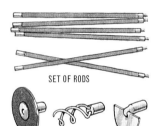

SET OF RODS

PLUNGER   CORKSCREW   SCRAPER

Drain rods

You may be able to rent a complete set of rods and fittings for clearing main drains. The rods come in 3-foot, 3-inch lengths of poly-propylene with threaded brass connectors.

The clearing heads comprise a double-worm corkscrew fitting, a 4-inch rubber plunger, and a hinged scraper for clearing the clogged section of drain piping.

MEASURING AND MARKING TOOLS

Tools for measuring and marking metal are very similar to those used for wood, but they are made and calibrated for greater accuracy because metal parts must fit with precision.

Scriber

For precise work, use a pointed hardened-steel scriber to mark lines on sheetmetal or a piece of steel or cast-iron pipe.

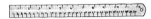

Center punch

A center punch is an inexpensive tool for marking the centers of holes to be drilled.

Steel rule

You will need a long tape measure for estimating pipe runs and positioning appliances, but use a 1- or 2-foot steel rule for marking out components when accuracy is required.

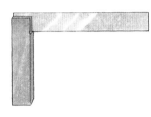

Try square

You can use a woodworker's try square to mark or check right angles; however, an all-metal engineer's try square is precision-made for metalwork. The small notch between blade and stock allows the tool to fit properly against a right-angled workpiece even when the corner is burred by filing. For general-purpose work, choose a 6-inch try square.

METAL-CUTTING TOOLS

You can cut solid bar, sheet, and tubular metal with an ordinary hacksaw, but there are tools specifically designed for cutting sheetmetal and pipes.

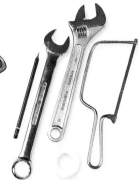

General-purpose hacksaw

A modern hacksaw has a tubular-steel frame with a light cast-metal handle. The frame is adjustable to accommodate replaceable blades of different lengths, which are tensioned by tightening a wingnut.

CHOOSING HACKSAW BLADES

You can buy 8-, 10-, and 12-inch hacksaw blades. Try the different lengths till you find the one that suits you best. Choose the hardness and size of teeth according to the type of metal you are planning to cut.

1 Raker set

2 Wavy set

Size and set of teeth

A coarse hacksaw blade has 14 to 18 teeth per 1 in; a fine blade has 24 to 32. The teeth are set (bent sideways) to make a cut wider than the blade's thickness, to prevent it jamming in the work. Coarse teeth are "raker set" (**1**), with pairs of teeth bent to opposite sides and separated by a tooth left in line with the blade to clear metal waste from the kerf (cut). Fine teeth are too small to be raker set, and the whole row is "wavy set" (**2**). Use a coarse blade for cutting soft metals like brass and aluminum, which would clog fine teeth; and a fine blade for thin sheet and the harder metals.

● **Essential tools**
Plunger
Scriber
Center punch
Steel rule
Try square
General-purpose hacksaw

Plumber's tool kit

● **Essential tools**
Hacksaw
Cold chisel
Tinsnips
Tube cutter

Hardness
A hacksaw blade must be harder than the metal it is cutting or its teeth will quickly dull. A carbon-steel blade will cut most metals, but there are high-speed steel blades that stay sharp longer and are less prone to losing teeth. However, being rigid and brittle, they break easily. Blades of high-speed steel combined with a flexible metal backing, called bimetal blades, are nearly unbreakable.

Installing a hacksaw blade
With its teeth pointing away from the handle, slip a new blade onto the pins at each end of the hacksaw frame. Apply tension with the wingnut. If the new blade tends to wander off-line as you cut, tighten the wingnut.

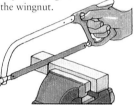

Turning a blade
Sometimes it's easier to work with the blade at right angles to the frame. To do so, rotate the blade-mounting pins a quarter turn before fitting the blade.

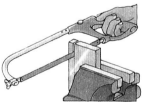

Turn first kerf away from you

Sawing metal bar
Hold the work in a vise, with the marked cutting line as close to the jaws as possible. Start the cut on the waste side of the line with short strokes until the kerf is about 1/16-inch deep; then turn the bar 90 degrees in the vise so that the kerf faces away from you and cut a similar kerf in the new face. Continue in this way until the kerf runs right around the bar, then cut through the bar with long steady strokes. Steady the end of the saw with your free hand and put a little light oil on the blade if necessary.

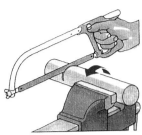

Sawing rod or pipe
As you cut a cylindrical rod or pipe, rotate it away from you until the kerf runs right around the work before you sever it.

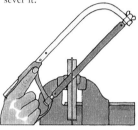

Sawing sheetmetal
To saw a small piece of sheet-metal, sandwich it between two strips of wood clamped in a vise. Adjust the metal to place the cutting line close to the strips, then saw down the waste side with steady strokes and the blade angled to the work. To cut a thin sheet of metal, clamp it between two pieces of plywood and cut through all three layers simultaneously.

Sawing a groove
To cut a slot or groove wider than a standard hacksaw blade, fit two or more identical blades in the frame at the same time.

Junior hacksaw
Use a junior hacksaw for cutting small-bore tubing and thin metal rod. The simplest ones have a solid spring-steel frame that holds the blade under tension.

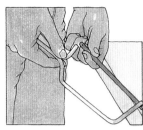

Fitting a new blade
To fit a blade, locate it in the slot at the front of the frame and bow the frame against a workbench until the blade fits in the rear slot.

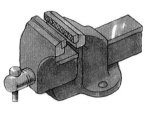

Metalworker's vise
A large metalworker's vise has to be bolted to the workbench, but smaller ones can be clamped on. Slip plastic or brass liners over the jaws of a vise to protect workpieces held in it.

Cold chisel
Plumbers use cold chisels for hacking old pipes out of masonry. They are also useful for chopping the heads off rivets and cutting metal rod. Sharpen the tip of the chisel on a bench grinder.

Straight snips

Universal snips

Tinsnips
Tinsnips are used for cutting sheet metal. **Straight snips** have wide blades for cutting straight edges. If you try to cut curves with them, the waste usually gets caught against the blades; but it is possible to cut a convex curve by progressively removing small straight pieces of waste down to the marked line. **Universal snips** have thick narrow blades that cut a curve in one pass and will also make straight cuts.

Using tinsnips
As you cut along the marked line, let the waste curl away below the sheet. To cut thick sheet metal, clamp one handle of the snips in a vise, so you can apply your full weight to the other one.

Try not to close the jaws completely every time, as that can cause a jagged edge on the metal. Wear thick gloves when cutting sheetmetal.

Sheetmetal cutter
Tinsnips tend to distort a narrow strip cut from the edge of a metal sheet. However, the strip remains perfectly flat when removed with a sheet-metal cutter. The same tool is also suited to cutting rigid plastic sheet, which cracks if it is distorted by tinsnips.

Tube cutter
A tube cutter slices tubing exactly 90 degrees to its length. The pipe is clamped between the cutting wheel and an adjustable slide with two rollers and is cut as the tool is moved around it. The adjusting screw is tightened between each revolution.

Pipe and tubing can also be cut with a hacksaw or reciprocating saw.

Chain-link cutter
Cut large-diameter cast-iron pipe with a chain-link cutter. Wrap the chain round the pipe, locate the end link in the clamp, and tighten the adjuster until the cutter on each link bites into the metal. Work the handle back and forth to score the pipe and continue tightening the adjuster intermittently until the pipe is severed.

Metal hole-punch kit

Another option for making holes is to use a metal hole-punch kit. This features a lever-activated hand tool, and dies and punches for creating holes in aluminum, brass, copper, plastic, and mild steel.

To use the hole-punch kit, first mark the hole location on the workpiece. Then, position the punch over the mark and firmly squeeze the handles together to drive the cutting die through the metal.

METAL BENDERS

Thick or hard metal must be heated before it can be bent successfully, but soft copper piping and sheetmetal can be bent while cold.

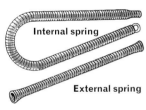

Internal spring

External spring

Bending springs

You can bend small-diameter pipes over your knee, but their walls must be supported with a coiled spring to prevent them from buckling.

Push an internal spring inside the pipe, or slide an external one over it. Either type of spring must fit the pipe exactly.

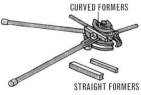

CURVED FORMERS

STRAIGHT FORMERS

Tube bender

With a tube bender, a pipe is bent over one of two fixed curved formers that are designed to give the optimum radii for plumbing and to support the walls of the pipe during bending. Each has a matching straight former, which is placed between the pipe and a steel roller on a movable lever. Operating this lever bends the pipe over the curved former.

Soft mallet

Soft mallets have a head made of coiled rawhide, hard rubber or plastic. They are used in bending strip or sheetmetal, which would be damaged by a metal hammer.

To bend sheetmetal at a right angle, clamp it between straight boards along the bending line. Start at one end and bend the metal over one of the boards by tapping it with the mallet. Don't attempt the full bend at once, but work along the sheet, increasing the angle gradually and keeping it constant along the length until the metal lies flat on the batten. Tap out any kinks.

TOOLS FOR JOINING METAL

You can make permanent watertight joints with solder, a molten alloy that acts like a glue when it cools and solidifies.

Mechanical fasteners such as compression joints, rivets, and nuts and bolts are also used for joining metal.

SOLDERS

Solders are special alloys for joining metals and are designed to melt at temperatures lower than the melting points of the metals to be joined. Soft solder melts at 365°F to 482°F. Brazing, a method of hard soldering involving a copper and zinc alloy, requires the even higher temperature of 1562°F to 1832°F.

Solder is available as a coiled wire or a thick rod. Use soft solder for copper and brass plumbing fittings and pipe.

FLUX

To be soldered successfully, a joint must be perfectly clean and free of oxides. Even after the metal has been cleaned with steel wool or emery cloth, oxides form immediately, making a positive bond between the solder and metal impossible. Flux is used to form a chemical barrier against oxidation.

Corrosive or "active" flux, applied with a brush, dissolves oxides but must be washed from the surface with water as soon as the solder solidifies, or it will go on corroding the metal.

A "passive" flux, in paste form, is used where it is impossible to wash the joint thoroughly. Although it does not dissolve oxides, it excludes them adequately for soldering copper plumbing joints and electrical connections.

Another alternative is to use wire solder containing flux in a hollow core. The flux flows just before the solder melts.

Soldering irons

For successful soldering, the work has to become hot enough for the solder to melt and flow—otherwise it solidifies before it can completely penetrate the joint. A soldering iron is used to apply the necessary heat.

Pencil-point iron

Tapered-tip iron

At one time, soldering irons were simply heated in a fire, but today's electric versions are far handier to use because the temperature is both controllable and constant.

Use a low-powered pencil-point iron for soldering electrical connections. To bring sheetmetal up to working temperature, use a larger iron with a tapered tip.

For more control and versatility, choose a trigger-activated soldering gun. These often have two wattage ranges, the lower for fine work and the higher for heavier jobs.

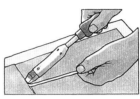

Tinning a soldering iron

The tip of a soldering iron must be coated with solder to keep it oxide-free and maintain its performance. Clean the cool tip with a file; then heat it to working temperature, dip it in flux, and apply an even coat of solder.

Using a soldering iron

Clean the mating surfaces of the joint to a bright finish and coat them with flux, then clamp the joint tightly between two wooden strips so it does not move out of position. Apply the hot iron along the joint to heat the metal thoroughly, and then run its tip along the edge of the joint, following closely with the solder. The solder flows immediately into a properly heated joint.

Gas torch

Even a large soldering iron can't heat thick metal fast enough to compensate for heat loss from the joint, and this is very much the situation when you solder copper pipe. Although the copper unions have very thin walls, the pipe on each side dissipates so much heat that a soldering iron cannot get the joint itself hot enough to form a watertight soldered seal. Instead, use a gas torch with an intensely hot flame to heat.

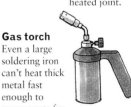

Reseating tool

If the seat of a tap has become so worn that even fitting a new washer won't produce a perfect seal, use a reseating tool to grind the seat flat.

Remove the tap's faucet handle, stem, and stem nut, then screw the cone of the reseating tool into the faucet valve cavity. Turn the knurled adjuster to lower the cutter onto the worn seat, and then turn the bar to grind the seat.

● **Essential tools**
Bending springs
Soft mallet
Soldering iron
Gas torch

Plumber's tool kit

Gas torch (continued)
the work quickly. The torch runs on propane or MAPP gas contained under pressure in a disposable metal canister that screws onto the gas inlet. Open the control valve and light the gas released from the nozzle, then adjust the valve until the flame roars and is bright blue. Use the hottest part of the flame—about the middle of its length—to heat the joint.

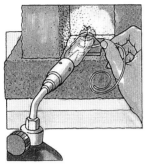

● **Essential tools**
Open-end wrenches
Adjustable wrench

Hard soldering and brazing
Use a gas torch for brazing and hard soldering. Clean and flux the work—if possible with an active flux—then wire or clamp the parts together. Place the assembly on a fireproof mat or surround it with firebricks. Bring the joint to red heat with the torch, then dip a stick of the appropriate alloy in flux and apply it to the joint.
When the joint is cool, chip off hardened flux, wash the metal thoroughly in hot water, and finish the joint with a file.

Fireproof mat
It's a good idea to buy a special fireproof mat from a plumbing-supply outlet to protect flammable surfaces from the heat of a gas torch.

Smooth-jaw adjustable wrench
This older-style wrench is ideal for gripping and manipulating chromed fittings because its large smooth jaws will not damage the surface of the metal.

Heat gun
Some heat guns designed for stripping paint can also be used for thawing frozen pipe. You can vary the temperature of an electronic gun from about 200°F to over 1000°F. A heat shield on the nozzle reflects the heat back onto the work.

WRENCHES
A professional plumber uses a great variety of wrenches on a wide range of fittings and fasteners. However, there is no need to buy them all, since you can rent ones that you need only occasionally.

Open-end wrench
A set of open-end wrenches is essential for a plumber or metalworker. In many cases, pipes run into a fitting or accessory, and the only tool you can use is a wrench with open jaws.
The wrenches are usually double-ended and combine two sizes. In some sets, the sizes are duplicated so you can turn two identical nuts simultaneously, as when tightening or loosening a compression joint, for example.

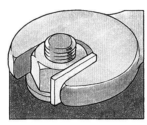

Achieving a tight fit
A wrench must be a good fit or it will round the corners of the nut. In an emergency, pack out the jaws with a thin shim of metal if you don't have the right wrench for the job.

Box-end wrench
The closed head of a box-end wrench is stronger and fits better than an open-ended tool.

Square nut   **Hexagonal nut**

Choosing a box-end wrench
Choose a twelve-point wrench for speed and the ability to handle both square and hexagonal nuts. A six-point wrench, however, grips a hexhead fastener more securely. You can buy combination wrenches that have one closed end and one open end.

Socket tube
A socket tube is a steel tube with hexagonal ends. The turning force is applied with a bar slipped through holes drilled in the tube. Don't use a very long bar. Too much leverage may strip the thread of the fitting or distort the walls of the tube.

Adjustable wrench
An adjustable wrench, with its movable jaw, is not as strong as an open-end or box-end wrench, but it is often the only tool that will fit a large or painted nut. It's also ideal when an odd-size fastener is encountered. Make sure the spanner fits the nut snugly by rocking it slightly as you tighten the jaws; grip the nut with the back of the jaws. If you use just the tips, they can spring apart slightly under force and the wrench will slip.

Basin wrench
A basin wrench provides under-the-sink access to the nut that holds a sink faucet to the counter. It has a pivoting jaw that can be set for either tightening or loosening.

Radiator wrench
Use this simple wrench, made from hexagonal-section steel rod, to remove radiator drain plugs. One end is ground to fit plugs that have square sockets.

Pipe wrench
The adjustable toothed jaws of a pipe wrench are for gripping pipe and fittings. As force is applied, the jaws tighten.

Chain wrench
A chain wrench does the same job as a pipe wrench but can be used on pipe and fittings with a very large diameter. Wrap the chain tightly around the work and engage it with the hook at the end of the wrench, then lever the handle toward the toothed jaw to apply turning force.

Strap wrench
With a strap wrench you can disconnect a tub spout or other chromed fitting without damaging its surface. Wrap the strap around the pipe, pass its end through the slot in the head of the tool, and pull it tight. Levering on the handle rotates the pipe.

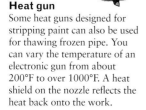

Locking pliers
Locking pliers clamp onto the work. They grip round stock or damaged nuts and are often used as a small clamp.

Plumber's tool kit

FILES

Files are used for shaping and smoothing metal components and removing sharp edges.

CLASSIFYING FILES

The working faces of a file are composed of parallel ridges, or teeth, set at about 70 degrees to its edges. A file is classified according to the size and spacing of its teeth and whether it has one or two sets of teeth.

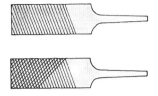

A single-cut file has one set of teeth virtually covering each of its faces. A double-cut file has a second set of identical teeth crossing the first at a 45-degree angle. Some files are single-cut on one side and double-cut on the other.

The spacing of teeth relates directly to their size: the finer the teeth, the more closely packed they are. Degrees of coarseness are expressed as number of teeth per 1 inch. Use progressively finer files to remove marks left by coarser ones.

File classification:

Bastard file–coarse grade (26 teeth per 1 inch), used for initial shaping.
Second-cut file–medium grade (36 teeth per 1 inch), used for preliminary smoothing.

Flat file

A flat file tapers from its pointed tang to its tip, in both width and thickness. Both faces and both edges are toothed.

Hand file

Hand files are parallel-sided but tapered in their thickness. Most of them have one smooth edge for filing up to a corner without damaging it.

Half-round file

This tool has one rounded face for shaping inside curves.

Round file

A round file is for shaping tight curves and enlarging holes.

Square file

Square files are used for cutting narrow slots and smoothing the edges of small rectangular holes.

Triangular file

Triangular files are designed for accurately shaping and smoothing undercut apertures of less than 90 degrees.

Needle files

These are miniature versions of standard files and are made in extra-fine grades. Needle files are used for precise work and to sharpen brace bits.

FILE SAFETY

Always install a wooden or plastic handle on the tang of a file before you use it.

1 Installing a file handle

If an unprotected file catches on the work, then the tang could be driven into the palm of your hand. Having installed a handle, tap its end on a bench to tighten its grip **(1)**.

2 Knock a handle from tang

To remove a handle, hold the blade of the file in one hand and strike the ferrule away from you with a block of wood (2).

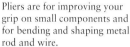

Cleaning a file

Soft metal tends to clog file teeth. When a file stops cutting efficiently, brush along the teeth with a fine wire brush called a file card, then rub chalk on the file to help reduce clogging in future.

PLIERS

Pliers are for improving your grip on small components and for bending and shaping metal rod and wire.

Slip-joint pliers

For general-purpose work, buy a sturdy pair of slip-joint pliers. The toothed jaws have a curved section for gripping round stock, and most models have a shear for cutting wire.

Tongue-and-groove or waterpump pliers

The special feature of tongue-and-groove pliers is a movable pivot for enlarging the jaw spacing. The extra-long handles give a good grip on pipes and other fittings.

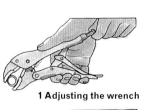

1 Adjusting the wrench

2 Releasing the wrench

Woodworking tools

A plumber needs a set of basic woodworking tools in order to lift floorboards, notch joists for pipe runs, and other odd jobs.

● **Essential tools**
Locking pliers
Second-cut and smooth flat files
Second-cut and smooth half-round files

Using locking pliers

To close the jaws, squeeze the handles while slowly turning the adjusting screw clockwise **(1)**. Eventually the jaws will snap together, gripping the work securely. To release the tool's grip on the work, pull the release lever **(2)**.

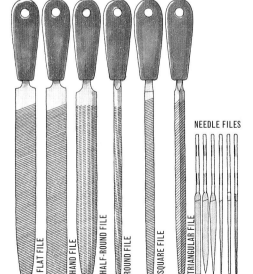

NEEDLE FILES

FLAT FILE | HAND FILE | HALF-ROUND FILE | ROUND FILE | SQUARE FILE | TRIANGULAR FILE

Glossary

A

ABS pipe
Acrylonitrile butadiene styrene pipe, a plastic pipe used in plumbing systems.

Air lock
A blockage caused by trapped air, as in a pipe.

Aquastat
A device for regulating the temperature of water.

B

Back-siphon
The flowing back of used or polluted water from a plumbing fixture into the pipe which feeds it; due to reduced pressure in the pipe.

Bleed valve
A valve on one side of a radiator that is loosened to purge air

Blower
The part of a forced-air heating system that circulates air.

Bore
The hollow part of a pipe or tube, also, to drill a hole.

Burner
The component of a furnace that burns oil or gas to heat air or water.

Burr
The rough, raised edge left on a pipe or other workpiece after cutting or filing.

C

Cap-nut
The nut used to tighten a fitting onto pipework.

Circulator pump
A motorized device that controls the flow of water to the radiators or convectors in a hot-water heating system.

Cleanout
A removable plug in a drainpipe or trap that allows access to the pipe in order to clear out blockages.

Cowl
A chimney covering which helps to control airflow.

CPVC
Chlorinated polyvinyl chloride, a plastic pipe used in water supply lines.

Creosote
A flammable, tarry substance, exuded from burning wood, that forms on the inside walls of chimneys.

D

Damper
A paddle-like device inside an air duct that regulates airflow to different parts of a house in a forced-air system.

Dielectric union
A special connector used to join copper and steel pipe. It prevents the electrolytic reaction that causes corrosion when these dissimilar metals are joined together.

Duct
A metal passageway that carries air to and from the furnace in a forced-air heating system.

DWV
Drain-Waste-Vent. The part of a plumbing system that carries away waste water.

E

Expansion tank
A cylinder attached to a boiler that relieves the excess pressure created when water in a hot-water heating system heats and expands.

F

Ferrule
A supportive sleeve or ring encircling a pipe, or joint.

Fire surround
A nonflammable metal or ceramic structure, often decorative, surrounding a fireplace.

Fixture
In plumbing terms, a device, such as a bathtub or toilet, that is served by water pipes.

Flue
The chimney pipe or other passageway which carries smoke to the outer air.

Flux
A paste used in soldering that assists in the fusion of one metal to another.

G

Galvanized
Covered with a protective coating of zinc.

Ground

A connection, as a wire, or rod, that provides a path of least resistance connecting electricity with the earth, providing a safety feature.

H

Humidistat
An device that measures and regulates the degree of humidity.

I

I-beam
An I-shaped steel supporting beam.

Insulation
Materials used to reduce the transmission of heat or sound. Also, nonconductive material surrounding electrical wires or connections to prevent the passage of electricity.

L

Level
To make perfectly horizontal or vertical. Also, an instrument, with a visible bubble of liquid, which measures the level quality of a structure.

O

Overflow pipe
A drainage pipe designed to safely discharge water that has risen above its intended level in a water heater.

Oxidize
To form a layer of metal oxide, as in rusting.

P

PB pipe
Polybutylene pipe, formerly used in plumbing systems, now outdated but still found in some older homes.

Penetrating oil
A thin lubricant which will seep between corroded components.

PEX
Cross-linked polyethylene, a pipe used in plumbing, mainly for in-floor radiant heat systems.

Plumb

To check the vertical aspect of a workpiece or structure for level. Also, a weighted line used to check the vertical.

Polyethylene
A moisture-resistant, lightweight plastic.

PVC
Polyvinyl chloride, a plastic pipe in plumbing systems.

R

Rust inhibitor
A chemical added to water in a boiler in order to keep the pipes in a hot-water heating system from corroding.

S

Septic tank
A sewage-storage tank in which waste is broken down into bottom sludge, surface scum, and gray water, which is discharged into a leach field.

Sillcock
A stem-and-seat faucet with a long stem typically installed as an outdoor faucet. Freezeless sillcocks may be left on during freezing weather.

Solder
The process of heating metal to a fluid state and fusing metal pieces together.

T

T&P relief valve
A regulating valve in a water heater which opens to release pressure.

Thermostat
A temperature-regulating mechanism.

Trap
A bent section of pipe in a plumbing system, below a bath, sink, etc., which holds standing water to prevent the passage of gases.

V

Vent
A device that permits air to bleed out automatically as a steam radiator heats up.

VOM
Volt-ohmmeter, a device which measures electrical resistance in ohms.